Grits is Groceries

Published by
Southland Press, Inc.
2755 Ebenezer Rd. SE
Conyers, GA 30094

Darrell Huckaby
Grits is Groceries
and other facts of Southern life
Copyright   2000, 2006
Printed in the United States of America
Second Edition

Text Design by Lisa Huckaby
Cover Design by Don Smith--The Adsmith, Athens GA

ISBN   978-1-4243-2195-7

Grits is Groceries

and
other facts of
Southern life

Darrell Huckaby

Acknowledgments

This book has been a labor of love and is the fulfillment of a dream I've had longer than I care to admit. There are many people responsible for this dream coming to fruition, and I would like to offer a word of acknowledgment and heart felt thanks to each of them.

First, I would like to thank my father, Homer Huckaby, who taught me to love the written word, and my mother, Tommie Huckaby, who provided me with a rich larder of childhood memories upon which to draw inspiration for my stories.

I would be remiss if I didn't acknowledge the dedicated teachers I had at Porterdale School and Newton County High School. They played a major role in shaping my life.

I offer my love, and my thanks, to my wife, Lisa, who has offered me encouragement and support throughout this project and who has spent countless hours, herself, helping to turn *Grits* into a reality. I also extend a special thanks to our children--Jamie, Jackson, and Jenna--and a word of apology for not being as attentive as I should have been while this book was being prepared for press.

I can think of no person more instrumental in the publication of this book than the little lady from Montezuma--Alice Queen--editor of the *Rockdale Citizen*. I thank her for giving me a forum in which to share my thoughts and feelings. Without her faith in my talents and abilities, *Grits is Groceries* would not exist.

And lastly, to my readers, whose kind response to my weekly column provided me with the impetus to publish this collection.

Thank you all, and may God bless.
Darrell Huckaby

For

Homer Huckaby

1

I'm as Southern as Cotton . . . or grits ain't groceries

I'm as Southern as Cotton . . .

I'm Southern. Make no mistake about it. I'm as Southern as cotton, and proud of it. I was raised in a Georgia mill village, educated in a large Southern university, and have been a lifetime member of the Methodist church. You can't hardly get any more Southern than that.

Barbecue, corn bread, slow cooked vegetables, seasoned with pork, and all manner of battered and fried meats have been and continue to be a part of my diet. Sweet iced tea is a given. I eat dinner in the middle of the day and supper in the evening. Yes, I grew up putting peanuts in my Coca Cola.

I don't live off the land, but I fully understand the attraction for those that do. I don't have a pickup truck or a hound dog or a shotgun, but most of my relatives have all of the above.

I will never live anywhere that doesn't have a red clay motif and I never hope to live among people who don't understand why an inch of snow is a big deal. As far as I'm concerned, Nashville's up north, Florida is the Tropics, and Alabama is out west.

I know my manners. I hold the door open for ladies, take my hat off in the house, and always say "ma'am." I also say "mama" and "ain't" every once in a while. Of course I understand that "y'all" is a perfectly good contraction, always to be used in the second person plural.

I'm not still fighting the War Between the States (there was nothing civil about it), but appreciate those that did, enough to have named my only son Jackson Lee, without apologies to anyone.

I don't like anyone from above the Mason-Dixon line telling me how we should do things down here and I have little patience for those that sit and whine about how much better life was back in Buffalo. Last time I was there, there were no fences keeping folks out.

I know exactly why college football is the greatest

spectacle in the world and why pretty women cry and grown men hug total strangers when their team does good.

I hope all readers find a laugh in my book. You may find a tear or two.

Those of you who are as Southern as I am will enjoy this book. It will bring back precious memories of a bygone day. It will make you pause, if only for a moment, and remember how things used to be. It will also cause you to wonder how in the world things got to be how they are now. It will give you cause to celebrate your Southerness.

Those of you who "ain't from around here" might enjoy it, too. Hopefully it will help you gain a little insight into what makes us Southerners tick.

I say again—I'm Southern, and proud of it. In fact, if I ain't Southern, grits ain't groceries.

Facts Every Georgian Should Know

This column has been stolen by more internet pirates than any other I've written. But the words are still mine and the facts are still solid gold.

I can't help but notice that there are more and more people in our community that talk funny and turn their nose up at ham hocks and collard greens. Yankees in Georgia! How did they ever get in? As part of my civic duty I want to provide a primer, of sorts, of useful information these folks need in order to live comfortably amongst us. Here are some facts that every Georgian should know.

Coca Cola is ours and unless you've had one in a green tinted six ounce bottle with a slight crust of ice on it—you don't know what the real thing is.

If it weren't for a Georgian—Crawford Long of Jefferson—open heart surgery would hurt like hell.

True Georgians say "ma'am" and "sir" and call their mothers "mama" and their fathers "daddy." Y'all is a perfectly good contraction and never means just one person, and if y'all don't like the way we talk, Delta (which is also ours) is ready when y'all are.

Long before the Olympics brought the world's greatest athletes to Atlanta, we gave the world Ty Cobb, Jackie Robinson, Walt Frazier, Luke Appling, Johnny Mize, Fran Tarkenton, Bobby Jones, Wyomia Tyus and Herschel Walker. If you don't know who those people are you need to find out before you go to bed. Long after the Olympics are forgotten the greatest tournament in golf will still be played in Augusta every April and 96,000 or so red and black faithful will gather for services on autumn Saturdays in Athens. No matter how many we play in, nothing will top the excitement of the first World Series or the first Super Bowl. Turner Field is nice, but I still miss Ponce De Leon Park.

The Stone Mountain carving is LOTS bigger than the one on Mt. Rushmore, and the people honored on it deserve to be. It wasn't just about slavery.

Atlanta was called "the city too busy to hate" during the civil rights era of the 60s because it was, and we should be proud of that.

In 1864 Sherman burned Atlanta, and much of Georgia, on his way to the sea. Crack cocaine is doing more damage in Atlanta than Sherman ever did.

We don't grow the most peaches, but still deserve to be called the *Peach State*, because ours are the best. We do produce the most peanuts, pecans, and poultry.

Elvis wasn't ours, but Otis Redding, James Brown, the Almond Brothers, Johnny Mercer, Joe South, Ray Charles, Bill Anderson, Brenda Lee, Trisha Yearwood, and Alan Jackson are.

So are Sidney Lanier, Joel Chandler Harris, Margaret Mitchell, and Lewis Grizzard. Find something these folks have written and start reading. I'll bet my next cotton crop you're hooked for life.

FDR adopted us. His "Little White House" in Warm Springs is exactly as it was the day he died there, near the end of

WW II. Every Gerogian needs to visit Warm Springs. FDR's New Deal put Georgians to work and turned an entire generation of our people into "Yellow Dog Democrats." Depression era Georgians would vote for a yellow dog if it were running on the Democratic ticket.

Georgia once had three governors at the same time. Lester Maddox wasn't one of them, but was elected by the legislature without getting a majority of the popular vote. He did a great job, too. Zell Miller was the best governor I never voted for and Jimmy Earl Carter, whom we have to claim, was the worst president we ever had. But now he has all the answers to all the problems.

We finally did change the flag, and Sonny's looks way better than Roy's.

Gone With the Wind belongs to us. We own it. It's by one of us and about us. It's one of the world's great novels, an absolute film classic, and we don't need to apologize for liking it.

WSB means "Welcome South Brother"—but she ain't what she used to be. Neither is the Atlanta Constitution, by the way.

The Brown Thrasher, the Cherokee Rose, and the Live Oak are our symbols. Proud, decent people are our heritage. None of the above are as plentiful as they once were, but none are on the endangered list either.

The best barbecue in the world used to be at Fresh Air in Jackson or Sprayberry's in Newnan. Sprayberry's has gone downhill--but Pippin's, in Conyers, is just as good. Archie's in Darien and William's in Savannah are both history, so I'm looking for the best fried shrimp. The best catfish is still served at Henderson's in Covington, but I surely do miss Clarence. My mama's gone, and I haven't had fried chicken to compare to hers since she died. Hers was the best as sure as Grits is groceries. Sugar doesn't belong in cornbread and God intended for tea to be sweet. If you don't like these foods, you ought to consider moving.

And lastly—Georgia ain't heaven, but it will sure do 'til I get there.

"Accused" of Being Southern; Guilty as Charged.

If I live to be a hundred, I'll never understand why Yankees choose to live among us if life is so much better up north. I can't help but agree with the late Lewis Grizzard when I run across folks like the lady in this column. "Delta is ready when you are, y'all"

In a bizarre incident at the local post office last week, I was "accused" of being Southern. That's right. I wasn't called Southern, I was accused of it. There's a big difference.

I was standing in line behind a rather innocuous looking older lady. Suddenly, she went off on me. She screamed at me to back off and give her more space. Then she plunged the proverbial dagger into my heart. She said, "You're a Southerner, and I'm tired of all this cozy Southern (word that can't appear in the newspaper unless written by Dave Baker.)

I was stunned. Dozens of retorts came to my mind. Thankfully none of them found their way out of my mouth. Instead of retaliating, I did what any other well mannered Southern gentleman, who had been educated in a large Southern university and raised in the Methodist Church, would have done. I politely backed off and said nothing. However, I could not, for the life of me, get the incident out of my mind. I just didn't enter the post office in Conyers, Georgia, expecting to get attacked for being Southern.

My thoughts lingered on the lady's words and I began to wonder, "What, exactly, makes a person Southern?" The obvious answer is living in the South, but we all know that living in the South doesn't make a person Southern any more than living in Alaska makes a person an Eskimo. Got to be more to it than that.

OK. Being born and raised in the South would do it. Nope. I know people who have lived here all their lives who are about as Southern as cream cheese and bagels. Being Southern is not about location or geography. With the blending of culture that has occurred in our great nation over the past three decades, as more and more Americans get the good sense to move to the Sun Belt, Southern has now become a state of mind.

Let me tell you what Southern is.

Southern is saying "yes, ma'am" and "no sir." It's being able to unashamedly talk about your "daddy" and your "mama" instead of your "mother" and "father," or even your "mom" or "dad." If you can't bring yourself to say "mama" you might as well be from New Jersey. It's also, of course, using "y'all" freely and throwing "ain't" into a sentence occasionally, even though you know better.

Southern is the art of slowing down, which, unfortunately, is quickly becoming a lost art, even in the South. It's taking time from a hectic schedule to sit on the porch and visit for a spell. It's bringing home cooked food to a house where there has been a death, and staying long enough to make sure that everyone has had plenty and the dishes are washed.

Southern is wearing overalls without thinking of yourself as cute or as making a fashion statement. It's insisting that your daughter doesn't wear white shoes to church after Labor Day, no matter what the temperature is outside. It's feeling natural in a baseball cap with a heavy equipment logo and it is knowing not to comment on someone's clothes, because they may be the best they can afford.

Southern is grits, fried chicken, cornbread, peas, collards, pulled pork barbecue, and sweet iced tea.

Southern is understanding why college football is life or death and that the NFL is something to pass the time of day, but not anything to get worked up over.

Southern is being enough of a stock car fan to remember when Fireball Roberts crashed into the wall at Daytona, and it's turning up one's nose at the current interest in race car drivers by corporate America and all the new found fans who watch the cars run because it's a trend.

Southern is not wanting to refight "The War," but still being able to understanding why Robert E. Lee and Stonewall Jackson are heroes.

Southern is thinking that the people on the Andy Griffith Show reruns are just like the folks you grew up with.

Southern is going to church on Sunday and feeling funny when you head to the mall or the lake or the golf course instead. It's knowing all the words to the old gospel hymns and wondering why the song leader picks all the new fangled songs every Sunday instead of Amazing Grace and the Old Rugged Cross. Southern is driving to the cemetery and standing with the family beside the open grave, even if it's cold or rainy or you're late getting back to work. And it's pulling off on the side of the road when you meet a funeral, even though you don't know the deceased.

Southern is waving at cars that drive by while you're walking on the side of the road. It's smiling at strangers and hugging your friends. I guess Southern must be accidentally standing too close to someone in the post office. Or maybe it was the fact that I smiled at someone I didn't know.

Whatever the case, I am guilty as charged. I think the penalty for being caught being Southern is a weekend of eating barbecued ribs and boiled peanuts while watching three college football games in a row. Let the punishment begin!

The Name's the Game

If you ever find yourself overcome with boredom and need something to do, find a Georgia road map and study all of the colorful, interesting, and unusual place names. Many, such as Hiawassee and Chattahoochee, are beautiful Indian words. Many places are named for people long forgotton, and some are down right common. But a few stories about how Georgia towns got their names are real doozies.

I get many unusual phone calls from many unusual people in many unusual places. I suppose this is only fitting, since I'm a bit unusual myself. I got a call the other day from LuLu Bo Bo of

TyTy. She wanted me to come to her civic league luncheon and talk about the time Sherman marched through Georgia. In case you don't know, by the way, Ty Ty is in Tift County, which is way below the gnat line.

I told Miss LuLu Bobo that I would have to get back with her on my availability for the particular day she had in mind. However, her phone call did set me to thinking about all the colorful names that have been given to the towns and communities scattered across our state, and the origins of the names.

I've traveled all across this great state of ours on numerous occasions. I have been, as the saying goes, from Rabun Gap to Tybee Light and all points in between. I have a particular penchant for wandering off the main roads and exploring the lesser known highways—the little lines on our state road map. It's a good way to meet folks. During my travels I've found myself in some very interesting places with equally interesting names.

For instance, last spring I visited a community in northwest Georgia called Plum Nelly, because it is "plum" out of Tennessee and "nelly" out of Georgia. In the opposite corner of the state is a town called Fargo, because it is as far as one can go and still be in Georgia.

In northern Fulton County there is a community called Shake Rag. It got its name from the early days of railroad travel. If there was a need for the train to stop as it passed, so the story goes, someone would stand by the tracks and shake a rag to signal the engineer. When Eugene Talmadge was the scourge of Georgia politics he would often monitor election returns and one of his favorite expressions was, "Well, we've heard from the Shake Rag district. Now we can all go to bed."

If you take a trip down US Highway 25 through Bulloch County, in southeastern Georgia, you'll run smack dab into a place called Hopeulikit. This town got its name because the US postal authorities rejected several previous name proposals.

One of my favorite stories regarding the naming of a town is the one about Resaca, in northwest Georgia. In reality, this town was given its name by Mexican War veterans in honor of a great victory at Resaca de la Palma. The legend is much better. According to the story, a farmer had a quite homely daughter who couldn't seem to attract a beau. The old man offered a substantial dowry and finally got someone to take him up on his offer. To make sure the arranged wedding went off as planned, the man placed a bag over his daughters head before escorting her down the aisle. The preacher preformed the ceremony and then the old farmer lifted the bag off his daughter's face to allow the groom to kiss his bride. According to the story, the groom took one look at the girl and screamed, "Resack her," thus giving a new name to the farming community.

We have some pretty unusual towns with some interesting stories of their own in our part of the state. There's a community called Between over in Walton County, so named because it is between Monroe and Loganville.

Also in Walton County is the town of Social Circle. Social Circle supposedly got its name because a group of settlers, tired out from spending the day digging a town well, sat down to rest and began to pass around a jug. As the jug got emptier the men got rowdier. One man's wife, sent to check on the progress of the digging, is said to have remarked quite sarcastically, "Isn't this a social circle!"

Fire water is also said to have played a part in the naming of a town ten miles down the road from Social Circle. Again, according to legend, town organizers agreed to name the town after the man who stayed sober the longest at the celebration for settlement. The only teetotaler in the bunch, Mr. Mansfield, supposedly had the town named in his honor.

With all these unusual place names dotting the Georgia map, Conyers and Rockdale County seem downright boring. Conyers, of course, was named for Dr. Conyers, a Covington banker who bought the land for the railroad station and right of way. Our county was named for the Rockdale Baptist Church, so called because of the subterranean granite with which we're blessed.

I'm sorry to report that I could not accommodate Miss

Bobo's request to come to Ty Ty and talk about Sherman. I'm already booked that day—at the Methodist Church in Splitsilk.

How 'Bout a Pork Pig Sandwich?

I once met President George W. Bush and he asked me where to find good barbecue in Atlanta. I sent him to Harold's. But I had to ask him how he realized that I was a conniseur of good "Q". He said it was easy. He noticed the barbecue stain on my tie. If you know of a good place, "Don't tell me about good barbecue--take me to it."

A man stepped out of a pickup truck the other day and handed me a brown paper bag. "Got a little something for you," he told me.

You need to be careful when a man gets out of a pickup truck and hands you a brown paper bag. There's a real good chance the contents could be illegal, immoral, or intoxicating. I very carefully opened my gift and discovered, to my delight, that the content was none of the above. What it was was a T-shirt, from one of my favorite establishments—Sprayberry's Barbecue in Newnan.

The gesture was so thoughtful that I couldn't bring myself to complain that there wasn't a pork pig sandwich in the bag somewhere. Just seeing the shirt made my mouth water and my taste buds scream for some of the succulent hickory-smoked meat, drenched with the red nectar some people call barbecue sauce, and served with white bread and slaw. It's so good it would make a dog jump off a meat wagon, and you can quote me on that.

If you aren't from around here, you may not realize that discussing barbecue can be a dangerous proposition. Folks will get into a cuss fight quicker over barbecue than just about anything I can think of. In fact, barbecue ranks right up there with politics and religion when it comes to controversial discussion topics. Not only is it hard to reach a consensus as to where the best barbecue is served, there is no clear agreement as to what does and does not constitute or deserve to be called barbecue in the first place.

For instance, a very nice friend of ours, who can't really help being from Pittsburgh, recently invited my family over for a "barbecue." I was pleasantly surprised and couldn't wait to tie on the feed bag at my friend's house. Imagine my disappointment when I arrived in her back yard to find her husband roasting hotdogs and grilling hamburgers on a gas grill. Let's get one thing perfectly clear. Wienies ain't barbecue.

Neither, for that matter, is beef. My mother-in-law is a dear lady and affords me much better treatment than I deserve, but she has an unnatural aversion to pork. She won't eat it. I think it has something to do with the Yankee blood flowing through her veins. (Her mother was from Wisconsin, of all places.)

Anyway, my mother-in-law eats beef soaked in spicy red sauce and thinks she's eating barbecue. As long as we're setting things straight, let me make one thing perfectly clear. If it doesn't involve the north end of a south bound hog, slow cooked over hardwood coals for close to a day, it just ain't barbecue. If you don't believe me, look it up. It's in the Bible. I think it's in the 35th chapter of Deuteronomy.

Eating beef and calling it barbecue originated in Texas, I believe. You can't really hold it against them. Folks have to make do. I've been told that goat is the meat of choice at some Texas hoedowns. Please know that I have nothing against goats, but I won't knowingly go somewhere to eat one.

Memphis, Tennessee is famous for barbecued pork ribs. These do, of course, come from a pig, and I've been known to eat far more than my share of this delicacy. However, I've never been more disappointed than the time I went to the world famous Rendezvous Restaurant in Elvis's hometown. The ribs were rubbed with all sorts of seasonings and served dry. If I don't have to wash my face after eating ribs I might as well have eaten a hotdog, in Pittsburgh.

OK. Is everybody clear, now? Barbecue is pork, slow cooked over hot coals, and dripping with sauce. By the way, it should be pulled from the bone or chopped on a wooden board with a cleaver. Sliced doesn't count. I'm not completely inflexible, however. The sauce can be vinegar or tomato based.

Now that we've decided what barbecue is, let's talk about where to eat it. There are thousands of places across the South that serve a more than passable pork plate. A good rule of thumb for selecting a barbecue joint is to check the parking lot. If there is an equal number of pickup trucks and luxury cars out front, it's a good sign. Harold's Barbecue, out by the Federal Pen, is a good example of such an establishment.

Avoid places that are too fancy or seem to put an unusual amount of stock in how well dressed the servers are. Having old men with crewcuts and tattoos behind the counter is a definite plus. If fried shrimp or pasta is on the menu, leave immediately.

I've eaten barbecued pork pig sandwiches from Tuscaloosa to Hahira and all points in between. My personal favorites are the previously mentioned Sprayberry's and the Fresh Air Barbecue in Jackson. It's a toss up. I don't know which I'd choose at gunpoint. I do know that I've got to stop writing now and go get something to eat.

If you think all this discussion of barbecue has made me hungry, just wait until I write about catfish!

Just a Little Slice of 'Catfish Heaven'

If there is anything that can raise a Southerner's ire quicker than the Great Barbecue Debate, it's a discussion about who serves the best catfish. We lost Clarence Henderson in 2006, but Henderson's is still 'Catfish Heaven' to me.

Let's talk about catfish. If you are a regular reader of this column you know that I am engaged in a never ending quest to stay in touch with my Southerness. You can't get more Southern than catfish. If sweet tea is the "Champagne of the South," as it has been called, then catfish, dredged in cornmeal and fried up until it is crisp on the outside, its sweet white meat tender and moist on the inside, is truly the "Nectar of the Southern Gods."

Catfish and me go back a long ways. My family used to have fish fries quite frequently. I remember watching the men-folk cook fish in a black cooker over a wood fire. Catfish was always the entree of choice. My mother's friend, Gladys Rogers, made a dish to go with catfish called "Hell-in-the-bowl." It con-sisted of diced tomatoes, finely chopped Vidalia onions, hot pep-pers, with the emphasis on hot (thus the name), and vinegar. It would make a puppy pull a freight train.

As I grew older I discovered restaurants and have spent the better part of the past three decades roaming the South in search of Catfish Heaven. Now, if you aren't from around here, let me fill you in on some particulars about finding a good place to eat catfish. To begin with, forget chain restaurants. Catfish needs to be eaten at a family-owned restaurant where the same person has been cooking the fish and dropping the hushpuppies forever. Pride is one of the main ingredients when you're cooking catfish and it's hard to obtain pride when you work by the hour for a national franchise.

There are a few other rules to go by. Check the parking lot. It should be about fifty-fifty with local cars and those from surrounding counties. You may certainly try a place with a paved parking lot, but gravel is much preferable.

Avoid places that are too fancy. Folks who spend time and energy trying to make a restaurant cute don't have time to do justice to the fish they are cooking. It's OK for a catfish place to have curtains on the windows, but not a necessity. By no means should they match the tablecloths. Not having tablecloths is a plus. The decor should be limited to framed slogans, plaques of appreciation from local athletic teams, and pictures of the owners' grandchildren.

If you walk into a catfish place and are not greeted with a friendly smile, leave immediately.   Look around the room.   If conversations are going on between tables, that's a good sign.   If the waitresses call customers by name, that's even better.   Don't be offended, or even surprised, if your hostess asks if you need to see a menu.   Most patrons are probably regulars and know it by heart.

About the menu.   It can have items besides catfish, just not too many of them.   Shrimp, steaks, cheeseburgers, even bar-becue, are all acceptable.   But the main feature needs to be cat-fish.   All-you-can-eat should be an option.   The catfish should be served with slaw, French fries, and, of course, hushpuppies.   If you're below the gnat line, cheese grits and slices of onions will come on the side.   If it's your first time in the place, order the catfish, with sweet tea to drink.

I've eaten catfish at scores of establishments across the South, including several in the immediate area.   The best catfish in the free world are served at Henderson's on Highway 36, just south of Covington.   It meets all the criteria listed above, and then some.

I've been eating with the Henderson family for most of my forty-some-odd years.   When I say family, I mean family.   Mr. Clarence Henderson, who started the business, passed away a few years back, but in my mind's eye I still see him, every time I walk into the place.   He's still walking among his guests, which is how he truly treated his customers—as guests—in his white apron, a pitcher of tea in one hand, a coffee pot in the other, a smile on his face, and beads of sweat on his bald forehead.

Mrs. Henderson has been standing behind the cash regis-ter for as long as I can remember.   She hasn't aged a day in over thirty years.   Son Clarence is still back in the kitchen, up to his elbows in cornmeal, frying the most delicious catfish this side of heaven.   Sometimes he's joined by his brother David.   Practicing law in town during the day doesn't stop him from cooking fish at night, just as teaching at Eastside High doesn't stop sister Clarice from being everywhere at once—taking orders, bussing tables, and passing out plates heaped high with hot food, which is consistently good, night after night, year after year.

I'm sure many of you have your favorite places to eat fish and I'm glad some of you settle for fish not cooked by Clarence Henderson. It's hard enough to get seated, as it is. But if you've never had catfish in a down home atmosphere—you ain't been in Dixie, yet. And if you know a place that serves better fish—take me to it. I'll have to taste it to believe it.

Flag Flap Decisions Should be Left to Southerners

Well Roy changed the flag--to something that looked like a DOT truck. Sonny got rid of that one. He didn't add the Southern Cross, but he did make it look like the Stars and Bars--which is good enough for me.

I 'spect I'll make just about everybody mad today. I'm fixin' to talk about the flag. Not the one we pledge allegiance to each day with it's fifty stars and thirteen stripes. That would be Old Glory. Washington carried it across the Delaware. Marines raised it on Iwo Jima. Neil Armstrong placed it on the moon. Car dealers fly it all day and all night. I'm not talking about that flag. I'm talking about the Georgia flag, which has come under fire recently because of the St. Andrews cross that adorns a full two-thirds of the banner.

Before I begin my comments on the flag, let me take you on a virtual tour of my living room. It has a fireplace against one wall with an oak mantle above it that my daddy-in-law made. A hand carved bald eagle adorns one side of the mantle. A bronze sculpture of Robert E. Lee and Stonewall Jackson, mounted on horseback and meeting for the last time in a glade at Chancellorsville is on the opposite end.

On the wall above the roll top desk my mother bought for me when I got married is a print of a guy about my age leaning against the Vietnam Wall in Washington D.C. My Eagle Scout Award and some Bert Adams camp patches I designed are in frames next to it.

One entire wall is a bookcase, filled with hundreds of books. Many are about American history, a subject I've studied all my life and taught for a great part of it.

There are other prints on the walls. One shows General Lee meeting the remnants of Pickett's division returning from a failed charge up Cemetery Ridge at Gettysburg. Another shows Lee and Jackson in church, heads bowed, tears rolling down their cheeks. There is a print of the Stone Mountain carving and other prints of Lee and Jackson individually.

The lump under the quilt in the corner, playing a video game, is my ten year old son. His name is Jackson Lee Huckaby. I think you get the picture.

I am an American. I am a Southerner. I am a historian.

I understand the events that led up to the War Between the States. I never refer to it as the Civil War; there was nothing civil about it. I understand the motives of the political leaders and I understand the motivation of the men who fought, on both sides. I also understand the motives of the men who added the Confederate battle emblem to the Georgia flag in 1956.

Please know where I'm coming from when I say that Georgia really does need to change her flag.

I know that many, many people want to keep the flag the way it is. Trust me. I truly understand how they feel. No one is more proud of being Southern than I am.

I know that Robert E. Lee, who served valiantly in the United States Army and turned down full command of that same body, fought not to preserve slavery but to defend his homeland. I am fully aware that the vast majority of Confederate soldiers believed that they were fighting for personal liberty and independence, not so their rich neighbors could continue to own slaves.

I know that most of the Georgians who favor keeping the flag believe it does represent their Southern heritage and not racism. Unfortunately, these well intentioned people are not aware of the flag's history, or, if they are, allow emotion to overcome logic when they make their arguments for keeping the flag.

The Georgia flag was changed to send a message to the Supreme Court that our state would defy its integration order. That's the end of the story. That's a fact, no matter how hard we wish it were otherwise. The Georgia General Assembly turned the Confederate flag into a racial symbol when they did that. The battle flag actually replaced three bars that were added to the flag by a state legislature full of Confederate veterans. They were representative of the Stars and Bars, the official Confederate flag, and were put there to honor Confederate soldiers. The 1956 lawmakers took away that heritage and replaced it with their symbol of hate and defiance. Those are the indisputable facts. A flag should represent all the people of a state, and a flag designed to promote a segregated society can never represent all our people. Think about it.

Now, having said that, let me say this. Last week this newspaper ran a column by someone named Lars-Erik Nelson. Nelson works for the New York Daily News. He called the Confederate flag a flag for "losers" and his column was full of disparaging remarks about Southerners who fought under the flag and those who honor it today. His column showed that he is completely ignorant of the facts surrounding our country's greatest tragedy and has no understanding, whatsoever, of the Southern psyche. Of course he calls for us to stop displaying all Confederate flags immediately.

I've got a message for Mr. Lars-Erik Nelson. We will change our flag in our own due time as soon as a majority of Georgians think through the issues and realize why it is the right thing to do. In the meantime, inflammatory remarks from his kind will only make people more determined not to change it. We don't need any hyphenated-named Yankee from New York tending to our business, and as for me, Lars-Erik Nelson can just kiss my rebel ass.

It's Time to Take a Stand . . .
for Sweet Iced Tea

*This column, to my surprise, drew more comment, from a
wider area, than just about any other. Everything is
changing in the South, and much of the change is not for
the better. Some things we just need to hold onto, and
sweet iced tea is one of those things.*

It disturbs me greatly to address this topic, but never let it
be said that I shirk my responsibility. It has come to my attention
that we in the South have a drinking problem. I'm not talking
about booze, although I'm sure the consumption of wine, beer,
and government whiskey has increased exponentially since moon-
shining went out of style. Our problem is worse than that.

We are losing the fine art of making sweet iced tea, and
are allowing many establishments to get by without serving it at
all. This is not a trivial matter, y'all. Drinking sweet iced tea is a
part of our culture and has been for generations. Losing our penchant for making and enjoying the drink that has been called the
"Champagne of the South" is just one more step toward losing
our distinctiveness. Pretty soon one won't be able to distinguish
Conyers from Omaha.

I was eighteen years old before I learned that every family in America doesn't drink sweet tea at every meal. My mama
made it the same way every night, forever. She would boil water
in a copper kettle and then pour it over a large tea bag into a
Corningware pitcher. After the tea steeped a while she would add
sugar, not quite a whole scoop, while the tea was still hot. It was
perfect, night after night, year after year. Of course I didn't appreciate it, just like I didn't appreciate country fried steak one night a
week, fried chicken at Sunday dinner, and either biscuits or cornbread every night.

When I ate supper with my friends their mama's served
sweet iced tea, too, and it always tasted pretty much like the tea at
our house. No one ever asked me what I wanted to drink. They

just filled up the glasses, that had once been jelly jars, with ice and poured the tea.

When I was eighteen my mama and daddy and I took an improbable trip to New York City. We got in our 1968 Buick and headed north. Twenty hours and two breakdowns later, we found ourselves on the outskirts of Manhattan Island. We got a room at the Holiday Inn in Jersey City. After freshening up from our long ride, we went down to the hotel restaurant to get a bite to eat. When the waiter asked for our drink orders, I naturally said I'd have iced tea.

The rather stuffy server informed me that they didn't serve iced tea. He acted a little bit like I had ordered a glass of curdled milk.

My daddy asked him if they served hot tea. The guy said that they certainly served hot tea. He then admitted, under great duress, that they had ice on the premises. Daddy ordered a pot of hot tea and three glasses of ice. He steeped the tea, added several packages of sugar, and poured it over the glasses of ice the waiter had reluctantly brought. Porterdale had come to town, and so had sweet iced tea.

When I went away to college my horizons were expanded somewhat. I began to accept the fact that if I traveled above the Mason-Dixon line and ordered tea to drink with my meal it would not be a satisfying experience. The tea would come unsweetened. Everyone knows that no amount of sugar in the world will adequately sweeten a glass of cold tea. Almost as bad, the tea will have only one or two ice cubes floating on top. Everyone also knows that the glass should be plumb full of ice before the tea is poured into it. Otherwise it gets too watery.

Everyone also knows, or should know, that when you order iced tea in a restaurant, refills are free. I almost started the War Between the States all over again at a Lum's in Washington D.C. one night when my waiter, a bowlegged fellow who spoke with a lisp, tried to charge me eleven dollars and a quarter for the seven glasses of tea I had consumed with my meal. The matter was eventually resolved, but even if I'm elected President of the

United States, I won't be able to eat supper at the Lum's down near the White House.

Well, folks up north can drink what they want with their meals. Far be it from me to tell them how to live. If my whole world was covered by snow six months out of the year, I probably wouldn't want ice in my drink, either. But when their customs concerning the South's standard drink infiltrate down here, we need to do something.

For years I have noticed that we are having a little bit of a problem concerning our tea consumption. More and more frequently I've been invited to people's homes where sweet tea is not served. I somehow manage to grimace and bear it. (I can't quite grin at no sweet tea.) I've ordered tea at local dining establishments only to be told that sweet tea was not served. No problem. I just don't go back to those places. I've learned to automatically order an extra glass of ice with my tea to combat the one floating ice cube practice. I've learned to cope.

But Sunday I had an experience that blew me away and brought the iced tea problem to a head. I was at a place I had never eaten. I was told that they did, indeed, serve sweet iced tea. When mine arrived it contained half a cube of ice and half a lemon and, worst of all, was full of shrubbery. My wife insisted it was mint, but I think the waitress plucked it right out of one of the potted plants hanging from the ceiling. The tea tasted like it came right out of a can. If it was sweet or freshly brewed, I'm a midget Russian astronaut.

Enough is enough. Sons and daughters of the South unite. Stand up for your heritage. Demand that sweet iced tea be served at all places, public and private, the way God and your mamas intended.

The next thing you know, we'll be drinking Perriere with moon pies instead of RC Colas.

2

No Matter Where the Road Leads . . . Georgia's always on my mind

No Matter Where the Road Leads . . .

I love to travel. Always have. My earliest travel experiences came in the back seats of several secondhand Buicks. My family usually went on vacation once a year and the destination was almost always Jacksonville Beach, Florida.

What great times those were! There were no interstates and, of course, no air conditioning--at least not in any of the cars we owned. To combat the heat, and to save on a night's lodging, we would set out for Florida in the wee small hours of the morning. I would sleep for a great portion of each journey.

We weren't as safety conscious in those days. There were no seat belts, of course, and I often slept on the back deck while my sister stretched out across the back seat. I can remember looking up through the glass behind me at the night sky, trying as hard as I could to spot theBig Dipper. Eventually the hum of the tires on the rough Georgia pavement would serenade me to sleep. Occasionally, I would be startled awake, or even thrown from my perch, when my daddy had to slam on brakes for an unexpected stop sign or to avoid hitting a possum.

My parents had a great time on vacation. They would sing the miles away and the fact that neither could carry a tune in a bucket did nothing to diminish their enthusiasm or their enjoyment. It was enough for them that they were on the road, traveling side by side, toward some hard earned and well deserved rest and relaxation. In fact, "Side by Side" was one of the songs they most frequently butchered.

Since our cars were usually old and not in particularly good shape, occasional breakdowns were part of the adventure. Usually the problem was no more severe than an overheated engine or a broken fan belt, but my daddy, who, like me, never met a stranger, spent the down time getting to know the locals who hung out at the service station in whatever town we happened to be in.

As I have grown older, I've had opportunities to travel

across a great portion of our great country. Some people carry pictures of their children with them when they travel. We carry our children. There is no better education than traveling the highways and byways of America, seeing the sights and talking to the people, up close and personal, if you will.

Wherever I go, I take my Southerness with me. Honesty compels me to admit that it usually shows, too. I'm certainly thankful for that. I wouldn't want anyone to think that this old mill village boy would try to put on airs when he got a few miles out of town.

When I get ready for a trip outside the South, I often think of the late Dean William Tate of the University of Georgia. Dean Tate thought that the world began and ended at the Georgia state line. He considered Florida the tropics and Alabama the far west. One day he was visiting with us in the lobby of Russell Hall and, for some reason, was all riled up and talking about how bad things were "up north."

I finally got up the nerve to ask him how much time he had spent up north. He looked at me with righteous indignation and replied, "Why son, I spent a week in Nashville one time."

I know just how he felt. Although I was born with a touch of wanderlust and love to travel whenever possible, the best part is always coming home.

This chapter is about experiences I've had away from home. I hope you enjoy.

Thanks for the Memories

I'm still teaching US History, now at Heritage High School--and I still try my best, every day, to make it come alive for my students.

My colleagues at Edwards Middle School and I took about three dozen of our students on a field trip last weekend. We went to Boston. Not the Boston in south Georgia, between Morven and Thomasville. The one in Massachusetts. The Boston of Paul Revere and Fenway Park and JFK. The Boston that's covered with snow on the Ides of March. The Boston that had northeast winds ripping through the clothing of our Southern bred children like they weren't wearing any. That Boston. Hey—it was warm last August when we planned the trip.

It was really a great trip. We saw more in three days than some natives see in a year, and being in the cold and snow was an adventure for our students. But as our plane landed at Hartsfield International Sunday night, I couldn't help but think about how field trips have changed. When I was in school our field trips didn't involved airports. I recall going to the sewage treatment plant once. In the second grade we packed a picnic lunch, boarded a yellow school bus, and visited the Grant Park Zoo. We also got to see the Cyclorama. My girlfriend accidentally dropped a candy apple over the railing onto the head of one of the soldiers in the diorama. Fortunately, it was a Yankee soldier. I took the blame and for punishment had to sit on the bus while the other children stopped at Tastee Freeze for ice cream on the way home. Ain't love grand?

My mother used to tell me a story about her class trip in high school. She was a child of the Depression and of a single mother with four children to raise and no work. Her class at Social Circle High went to Jacksonville Beach, courtesy of some businessmen in town who believed that, even in hard times, young people should be rewarded for hard work. According to the story I've heard since birth, my mother's class stayed in a rented house.

The chaperones did the cooking and the students—all twenty-one of them—played on the beach all day. As they were leaving for the trip my grandmother gave my mother all the money she had in the world to take on the trip for spending money. I believe it was a dime.

On their last night at the beach, the Social Circle Class of 1941 got to go to the boardwalk. My mama still had her dime. She spent a nickel for cotton candy and with the other nickel rode the Ferris Wheel and has testified many times that she had never seen a prettier sight than the reflection of the full moon on the ocean, as viewed from the top of the Ferris Wheel. She also recalls that she had never tasted cotton candy before and in her words it was "the best stuff I'd ever put in my mouth."

My grandmother never had much material wealth to share with her children, but with her last dime she bought my mother a million dollars worth of memories that have lasted a lifetime.

Our trip to Boston was a bit more extravagant than my mother's trip to the beach on the eve of World War II. It was certainly more educational than a trip to the sewage plant and more eventful than visiting the Cyclorama. We walked the Freedom Trail and reenacted the Boston Tea Party. We ate clam chowder and baked cod and toured the USS Constitution. We were very proud to discover that *Old Ironsides* earned her nickname because she was built from sturdy Live Oak, harvested on Georgia sea islands. We relived the Camelot years at the Kennedy Library and the witchcraft hysteria at Salem. We retraced the path of Paul Revere and stood by the rude bridge at Concord which bore witness to the *shot heard round the world*. But throughout the entire trip I couldn't help but wonder if our students' parents were buying them a lifetime of memories. I hoped so, because they had spent considerably more than a dime.

On the village green in Lexington we did an impromptu reenactment of the skirmish there between the Minutemen and the British Regulars. As I was explaining how the drama had unfolded, some 224 years earlier, I repeated the words of Captain Jonas Parker, first American to die in the Revolution. "Don't fire unless fired upon, but if they mean to have a war, let it begin here!"

I don't know who threw the snowball at that precise moment. But the ensuing snowball fight was probably the greatest battle to take place in Lexington since Paul Revere left town. As I sought cover and watched the faces of our students, glowing with excitement, I knew. They were making memories. They were learning, but they were also making memories—and memories last a lifetime.

Jekyll in Spring—A Little Slice of Heaven

We still visit Jekyll every spring and it is still my favorite place on earth. Once a playground for the filthy rich, now it is a treasure that we all can enjoy.

Jekyll Island—Even as you read this I'm enjoying a restful week at one of my favorite places on earth. Spring Break at Daytona or Ft. Lauderdale? Been there. Done that.   Panama City? They don't call it the "Redneck Riviera" for nothing. Walt Disney World? At this time of year? No thanks. I'll keep visiting the quiet little island that was once the playground of millionaires.

My wife's family has been camping on Jekyll Island during spring break forever. It's one of many wonderful traditions I married into. Another is hauling hay when it's 103 in the shade, but you have to take the rough with the smooth. Right?

The week we spend camping at Jekyll is the most relaxing week of my year. My family travels a lot. After most of our vacations we need a week off to rest and recuperate. But not this one.

There are accommodations to fit every life-style

and budget on this tiny little hideaway. We camp. In fact, we've pitched our tents on the same campsite each of the past eighteen years, except one. In 1992 we had a different priority. Now we celebrate a birthday at Jekyll each year.

Always an early riser, I get up most mornings and take a bike ride down to the beach to watch the sun slowly climb out of the Atlantic Ocean, signaling the beginning of another day in Paradise, Georgia style. The beach is isolated at that time of day. I'm alone with the sun and the water and a few gulls or pelicans. When I return to the campsite the coffee is ready and the campfire from the night before has been rekindled. At no other time or place is reading the morning paper so pleasurable. The others accuse me of riding to see the sunrise every morning just so I won't have to brew the coffee or build the morning fire, but that's not really true.

Our morning activities usually include a long bike ride. There are bike paths everywhere. Some go through the salt marsh on the northern end of the island. Others take the adventurous rider in front of the cottages once owned by the Rockefellers and the Carnegies and their like, through the woods past an alligator pond, or out to a state park on the secluded south beach. Spring comes early to this part of Georgia and azaleas and dogwoods abound. My favorite trail winds in and out of Live Oak trees that are hundreds of years old. Spanish moss hangs over the path and Cherokee Roses grow alongside. Deer, raccoons, rabbits and wild turkeys are common sights. The path winds along the bank of the Jekyll River and Sidney Lanier's Marshes of Glenn form a watery plain of a thousand shades of green on the other side. When the wind is right, we ride on the beach, reveling in the feeling of the salt spray on our faces.

Our bike rides are magical. We stop each day at the little airstrip and if we're lucky get to watch a small plane take off or land. It's fun to stroll along the docks at the marina and talk to the yachters about their adventures and various ports of call. We almost always walk out on the pier to see if the fish are biting and sometimes, if the water's warm enough, people are pulling a shrimp net in the sound. Stopping at the island's only drug store for an icecream cone makes the morning complete.

There are dozens of things to do in the afternoon. Sitting around camp reading paperback novels is high on the list. So is playing on the beach or digging for sand dollars at the oceans's edge. There are also kites to fly, frisbees and baseballs to throw, sand castles to build, and birds to watch. Beginning to get the picture?

Some people come to Jekyll to play tennis and golf. I got in eighteen holes myself Monday, but only because my son wanted to play. I have to admit I played well. Two over par! I would have shot better if it hadn't been for that blasted windmill hole.

Suppertime is the best part of the day. A couple of times a week we might venture out to a seafood restaurant, but nothing beats the smell of steaks sizzling on the grill or the sound of fish frying in deep oil or the taste of fresh boiled shrimp served up with corn on the cob and eaten outside as the sun begins to settle over the marsh.

Evenings are exciting, too. That is, if you call sitting around the campfire, reliving the days activities with people you love, exciting. Sometimes we sit and look at the embers and talk and sometimes we just sit and look at the embers. Finally we retire to the cozy warmth of our sleeping bags, happy and content as humans have the right to be.

The best part of Jekyll Island is the slow pace and the absence of the throngs of people that crowd other spring break destinations. I pray it stays that way. So if learning what a wonderful place it is has made you want to visit Jekyll in the spring, I have a suggestion. Get on I-75, and drive north!

A Postcard From the Beach

I fell in love with Myrtle Beach the first time my wife Lisa and I visited there. Now I go back every chance I get. I've made good friends there, like Dick Timmerman and his family. Playing in the surf and eating fresh seafood every night makes the Grand Strand a true vacation paradise.

North Myrtle Beach, South Carolina. As I write this, I am sitting on a balcony watching the eastern sky begin to turn red and gold as the sun climbs slowly out of the Atlantic Ocean. Yes. A cup of steaming hot coffee sits on the table beside me. What's the expression? Nobody said life is fair. This week, I get the bear. Normally, the bear gets me.

I have a confession to make. They say it is good for the soul. I am a two-timer. Everyone who knows me knows of my love for the red clay hills of the Georgia Piedmont. Alas, I have a second love. The low country of South Carolina. So far my love affair with the Grand Strand has been limited to short lived trysts—temporary flings, if you will. However, if any place on earth could tempt me to permanently leave my native Georgia, it would be this part of the world.

As long as I'm confessing, I'll make another. For a long time, I avoided going to Myrtle Beach. I had no interest in the place. I decided I didn't like it without even going there. I think it was because of the name.

Myrtle. It reminded me of a girl I went to grammar school with. Her name was Myrtle and I didn't like her. She was the one who always volunteered to take names when the teacher left the room. She wrote my name down in the third grade because I read a word aloud in my reading book while Miss Elizabeth Willis stepped down the hall to take a dip of snuff. Miss Elizabeth Willis paddled my backside when she got back to the room. Because of that I never liked Myrtle and never wanted to visit a beach that shared her name.

My wife, Lisa, had grown up camping at Myrtle Beach

and tried to talk me into going there on vacation the summer after we were married. I was adamant. I wasn't going. What would we do all day? Sit around on the beach waiting for someone to tell on me for reading out loud? For all I knew Miss Elizabeth Willis might have retired to Myrtle Beach. I could just see her there, in one of those old fashioned bathing suits with long pantalets and a skirt, lurking behind a beach umbrella, waiting to pounce out and paddle me. Nothing doing.

We went to the Outer Banks of North Carolina, instead. We had a wonderful time, too, until a hurricane decided to visit at the same time we were there. We were among thousands of people who were evacuated off the north end of the island. Since we had three days of vacation left, I consented to stop at Myrtle Beach. It was love at first sight!

That was seventeen years ago. Lisa and I have made over twenty-five trips back to the Myrtle Beach area since the first one. It's like a second home. We have stayed at places from Little River to Pauley's Island and all points in between, and haven't found an area of the beach we don't like. We've camped at state parks and private campgrounds, stayed at small mom and pop hotels and luxury condos. Every visit has been a little slice of heaven.

We've watched the area grow from a rather cozy resort area to a sprawling and seemingly endless stretch of All-You-Can-Eat seafood restaurants, beach shops, miniature golf courses, amusement parks, and high rise hotels, not to mention enough country music shows to make Branson and Nashville envious. Naturally there is shopping galore.

But the main attraction, for us, is the ocean. Fresh local seafood is a close second. I love the ocean and could sit and watch it all day long. That is, I could sit and watch it all day if I didn't enjoy getting in it so much. The thing I like best about Myrtle Beach is the fact that the ocean has waves. Great big waves that allow one to raise body surfing to a high art.

The other people here can have the golf courses, of which there must be a hundred. They can shop 'til they drop at Barefoot

Landing and Broadway at the Beach and the factory outlets. They can ride the rides at the Pavilion and dance the shag or visit the Bowery where the band Alabama, country music legends, got their start. I'm going to sit on the beach and read a book and play in the ocean. All day. All week. I might come off the beach in time to drive up to Calabash to eat some fish and shrimp and scallops. If I feel real energetic I might throw the frisbee with my ten year old son, or build a sand castle with my seven year old daughter. I might even walk up the beach with my wife and teenaged daughter, if I won't embarrass them too much.

Hey! Being at the beach is a tough job, but somebody has to do it.

Having a wonderful time. Wish y'all were here!

Life on the Road a Mixed Blessing

*I guess you can have too much of a good thing, after all.
As much as I enjoy travelling, I got a bit more than I
bargained for on this improbable trip through our
country's Eastern corridor.*

Somewhere on the East Coast—As you read this my family and I are loaded into our Dodge Caravan, headed up the east coast. Taking a tip from Dinah Shore, we are trying to see the USA, albeit not in a Chevrolet. We are in the early stages of an extended camping trip during which we hope to watch whales off the coast of Maine and eat fresh lobsters from roadside pots, view the majesty of Niagara Falls, fulfill a lifetime dream, of mine at least, by taking in the Baseball Hall of Fame at Cooperstown, New York, tour the Amish country of Pennsylvania and relive Picket's ill-fated charge on the battlefield at Gettysburg. We haven't decided what to do the second week.

My family has been fortunate enough to travel quite a bit together. Traveling with kids is a bit of a mixed blessing. Former

Alabama governor George Wallace once defined a mixed blessing as having your daughter come home at three in the morning,
carrying a Gideon Bible. So it is with traveling with kids—you
have to be prepared to take the rough with the smooth.

I've learned certain truths by seeing the country with my
family. For instance, there is an unwritten law that makes it impossible for any two children or a wife to be hungry or need to use
the rest room at anywhere near the same time. I've also discovered that to obtain the number of minutes a child can sit in the
back of a car without asking "are we there yet" one must take the
square root of the child's age divided by the number of hours sleep
the driver—always me in our case—was able to obtain the night
before, and then subtract the number of days you've been on the
road. As you can deduct, the number grows infinitely small, in
direct proportion to the driver's PQ—patience quotient.

Nonetheless, the open road has quite an allure for me and
I love visiting new places and creating new memories. My wife
says that I never meet a stranger, and I love the people we encounter on our journeys. Also, so many memorable things happen
when you travel. We are only two days into our current trip and
my diary is getting quite full. For instance, we stopped at the
South Carolina Welcome Center early one morning. We were too
early, in fact. The place didn't open for another hour and a half.

As I approached the locked door of the office, before I
realized that it was still closed, I noticed a rather threadbare gentleman get out of a fairly ragged old car. He shook the door of the
building a couple of times then put his head against the glass and
peered inside. Trying to be helpful, I told him that I believed they
had not opened yet.

"I need a map," was his quite matter-of-fact reply.

"I believe they'll be open in an hour and a half," I coun-
tered, pointing at the sign on the door.

"Guess I'll wait," he responded. "They want a durned
fortune for a map in a fillin' station these days."

I used the facilities, which weren't closed, and backed
out of my parking space. My new friend was sitting patiently on

a bench beside the door, waiting for 9 o'clock and a free map. I couldn't help but wonder which of us had our priorities in order.

I noticed two other trends during our first day on the road. For one thing, Conyers is not anonymous anymore. I try to talk to everyone I meet. Whenever you get in a conversation with a new friend—remember, I never meet a stranger—one of the first and safest questions is, "Where are you from?" I never say Atlanta. I always, in fact, say Porterdale, if my wife, Lisa, isn't in earshot. When she is, she makes me admit that we live in Conyers. Everyone has heard of Conyers, Georgia these days. The name seems to be burned into the collective minds of the nation.

The second thing I've learned is that it doesn't take long to leave home. On our very first evening we ate at a restaurant somewhere along I-95. I'm not sure of the town. I'm not even real certain of the state. It could have been Virginia or Maryland or Delaware. But I'm certain that they didn't serve sweet tea, and they thought that one cube of ice was enough for a whole glass. The waitress at the place we ate breakfast the next morning didn't even bother replying when I asked if they served grits. She just looked at me like I had two heads and walked away.

I'm not worried about starving while we're gone, however. We're cooking most of our own food and I smuggled a couple of cans of Spam into the food box. I'll survive, unless Lisa finds the Spam.

Keep watching this space to find out what life is really like above the Mason-Dixon Line.

Even in Maine—Georgia is On My Mind

For most of my life I had dreamed of vacationing along the rugged coast of Maine. It took nearly fifty years, but I finally made it. It was everything I had imagined, and more. The view from Cadillac Mountain is truly awe inspiring, but I don't think I'd choose it over my daily red clay sunrise.

Bar Harbor, ME—I'm not exactly sure how far it is from Conyers to Maine, but however far it normally is, it's twice that when you drive here with a wife and three kids. No matter how great the distance, it's well worth the trip.

I don't want to sound like I'm auditioning for one of those twelve dollar travel guides, but the only word that can adequately describe the rugged beauty of Maine's coast is spectacular. For over a hundred miles steep cliffs plunge downward toward rocky beaches that are washed with the deep blue water of the north Atlantic—the cold north Atlantic. I tried to go swimming at one of the few sandy beaches on Mt. Dessert Island, which is where Bar Harbor is located. I lasted about thirty-five seconds in water up to my ankles. My feet turned blue and shrunk from a ten-and-a-half to a seven. I was, however, smart enough to get out of the water, which is more than I can say for some Yankee Americans who were swimming around in the frigid bay like they were at Daytona Beach on the 4th of July.

When my family and I pulled into Bar Harbor I thought we were up north. It certainly looked that way on my map. Turns out we are actually "down east," according to Maine residents who are here on vacation. Of course, according to the folks who have driven up from Boston for the weekend, we are not in Bar Harbor at all. We are in "Bah Hahbah." These are the same people, by the way, who "pahk" their "cahs" in the "gahrahge." And they think I talk funny.

One thing they have here in Maine is the lobster pound. All along the highways there are little roadside stands serving lobsters. Pick out the ones you want and they drop 'em in boiling seawater for 20 minutes, then you're good to go. They sell lobsters up here like we sell boiled peanuts at home, and for about the same price. It pains me to admit it, but they are one up on us. Lobsters are way better than boiled peanuts.

The only thing more plentiful than lobsters in Bar Harbor are rude New Yorkers. I ran into a couple at a lobster pound. I saw them eyeballing my license plate as they pulled up behind me and got out of their shiny new Lincoln Continental. Now understand, these lobster pounds are casual. I was overdressed in my T-shirt and shorts. I mean at these places—no shirt, no shoes—no problem. These guys were in white oxford button-down shirts with power ties. They looked as out of place as a Baptist deacon at a liquor store.

Taking one more look at my car tag they ambled up behind me in line, grinning like a couple of mules eating briars. In a mock Southern accent, taken directly from a bad TV movie, one of them said, "Well shut my mouth. I believe you all is from Georgia, isn't you?"

I looked around rather pointedly and responded, "Well, there's only one of me here, but yes, I'm from Georgia."

Mr. Intelligent then asked, "Does you all have lobsters down in Georgia?"

At that moment my twenty-three years in the classroom served me well. I fixed him with my best teacher stare and after a long pause replied, "No, we don't. But we do have enough manners not to make fun of visitors."

The guy reacted like a sixth grader caught on the eighth grade hall with bubble gum and a water pistol. He fell all over himself apologizing. Trying to make amends, he asked me what I did "down in Georgia."

I told him I was Lieutenant Governor. I didn't think Mr. Taylor would mind and think of the story the guy had to tell his wife when he got home.

One of the best things we did here, other than eat lobsters and torment New Yorkers, was to go whale watching. We got on a boat and went thirty miles out to sea. Magnificent creatures, eighty feet long, swam alongside and under our vessel. We saw them leap into the air and dive majestically, their tails slowly disappearing beneath the surface. It was truly an awesome experience.

I was standing along the railing of the boat when I felt a strong hand on my shoulder and someone shouted into my ear, "How 'Bout Them Dawgs!" I quickly remembered that I was wearing a UGA baseball cap, turned backward against the wind. A fellow member of the Bulldog nation had found me on a boat, thirty miles off the coast of Maine.

Turns out that I was talking to a doctor from Columbus who had sat in the same seat in Sanford Stadium for the past thirty-eight years. Talk quickly turned to football and the good doctor reminded me that the beginning of fall practice was only two weeks away. I suddenly felt an urgent need to get off that boat and head south. Maine is a beautiful state, but it ain't where I want to be during football season.

Y'all watch for us. The "Lieutenant Governor" will be home soon.

3

There's No Place Like Home . . . where there is never a dull moment

There's No Place Like Home . . .
where dull moments never exist

The person who coined the phrase, "There's never a dull moment," must have had a home very much like ours. Imagine a family composed of two parents with two or three jobs each, three children, all three years apart and all involved in a wide array of school, church, and social activities, add an assortment of pets and friends, plus a dash or two of misadventure and you'll get a pretty accurate picture of the Huckaby household.

Sometimes life seems to revolve around soccer and basketball, other times around the crises of the week, and, at still other times, school activities and the social calendar. One thing is crystal clear--it always does revolve, and at a dizzying pace.

If you will indulge me, I'll introduce my family. My wife, Lisa Potts Huckaby, is a lifetime resident of Rockdale County. A graduate of Valdosta State College, now University, she worked 14 years as an obstetrics nurse before going back to school to become a nurse-midwife. She is my rudder and keeps me sailing a semi-straight course.

Our first child, Jamie Leigh, was born in 1985. She looks exactly like her mother and is intelligent and articulate. She sings and dances and spends hours on the internet.

Our son, Jackson Lee, was born in 1989. He is a typical boy and likes sports and outdoor activities and avoids baths like the plague.

Our baby, Jenna Elizabeth, is the wild one of the bunch. She came along in 1992 and seems determined to make us old before our time.

This chapter deals with our desperate attempts to be a

Is Atlanta Night life
Gone With the Wind?

*I learned my lesson. Lisa and I have gone back to spend-
ing our Friday nights in front of the fireplace with our
glasses of prune juice and a couple of good books.*

It seemed like a good idea when I planned it. An evening
in Atlanta with my lovely wife, Lisa. It had been a long time since
we'd enjoyed a night out on the town. With all our kids and all
our jobs, a big night for us is pizza in front of the fireplace and a
rented movie not produced by Disney.

I'd planned this night for months. *Miss Saigon* was coming to the Civic Center. We'd seen it once, but from the balcony,
a hundred thousand miles from the stage—or so it had seemed.
This time, the very day tickets went on sale I started calling the
box office. I wore out the speed dial on three phones, but finally
got through and secured choice seats. They weren't an arm and a
leg, either. They were an arm and two legs, but you only live
once. Right?

As our big night approached I could hardly wait. Lisa
would wear a black velvet skirt with sequins. We'd have an intimate candle lit dinner. It would be like the old days. We'd sit
with our faces close together—laughing, talking, enjoying a romantic Italian dinner. Then we'd take a stroll in the night air,
enjoy the play, and maybe even go to an out of way bistro afterward for coffee and something sweet. The night would be ours
and pure magic.

She wore denim. But, of course, she looks lovely in denim.
The first seven restaurants we tried in Buckhead had three hour
waits. The eighth seated us right away. Our server had long purple
hair, three earrings in each ear and wore too much makeup. He
was a nice enough guy, but he wore too much makeup. We did sit
with our faces close together. We had to. Punk rock music was

blaring at decibels that would rival a shuttle lift-off.

The menu wasn't exactly Italian, but we did recognize a couple of entrees. We placed our orders and waited patiently, hoping for the best and wishing we had an interpreter for the music. After thirty minutes, our server, who had now dyed his hair orange and added a fourth earring, informed us that the chef had taken ill and our meals would be delayed indefinitely. We opted for a different restaurant. The service at *The Varsity* wasn't bad, for a Friday night. The grease from the onion rings hardly stained Lisa's jeans at all.

After dinner we still had time to kill and decided to visit *Underground Atlanta* for a nostalgic trip back in time. *Underground* was a happening place in Atlanta back in the '70s. Blind Willie, the Ruby Red Warehouse Band, and a dozen other entertainers kept the streets rocking until the wee hours and the place was alive with college students, suburbanites out on the town, and conventioneers from Cleveland and Des Moines and hundreds of other cities. Last Friday night *Underground Atlanta* was a perfect example of what Atlanta must have been the day after Sherman left. After ten minutes, spent nervously strolling up and down the practically deserted streets, we decided to head for the Civic Center while we were still able.

The Atlanta Civic Center. There's another Atlanta icon left over from the days when the Regency Hyatt's twenty-two stories towered above the city. It was something to behold in it's day, but is now a little like a once glamorous movie star trying to look her best in a thirty year old gown that no longer fits. It's tattered and frayed around the edges and the once luxurious seats are a little rickety and threadbare. But our location was excellent! We took our places and eagerly awaited the first act of *Miss Saigon*.

Just before curtain time a couple came in and filled the seats in front of us, the only vacant seats in our section of the auditorium. She was a pleasant looking lady with a hairdo large enough to make an Alabama beauty queen jealous. He was six-six with the widest head I've ever seen on a human being. And they were so in love! They sat with their heads together all night long.

The play sounded great. If I could have seen any of it, I'm sure I would have thought the acting superb as well. In case you're wondering, we skipped the dessert and coffee. Next Friday night we'll be back to double pepperoni and extra cheese. I hope all the copies of *Old Yeller* aren't checked out.

Child's Play Can Bring Unexpected Joy

Jackson gave up his dream to be a soccer star and Jamie has given up her dream of being a Rockette and is a student in the UGA pharmacy school. Our youngest, Jenna? Either a brain surgeon or Radio City Music Hall. The jury is still out.

As a father of three, who knew everything there was to know about parenting, right up until my first child was born, I share this advice. Don't ever boast about what your children will never do, because as sure as gritsis groceries—they are certain to someday do whatever it is that you say they won't.

Case in point. Soccer. There was a time when I looked upon the sport of soccer with total disdain.   Those of my generation considered it a communist sport. We thought those who played it were renegades whose mothers probably dressed them funny. No way a child of mine would ever get near a soccer ball, much less play on an organized team.

I have a confession about soccer. The first soccer game I ever saw, I was the coach. I didn't know a cross from a corner kick, but the principal at Clarkston High School needed someone to coach the girls' varsity soccer team and I needed the money. We played the first half of our first game with twelve players on the field. My players tried to tell me I was in err, but I shushed them. At halftime the boys' coach came down and pointed out my mistake. How was I to know the goalkeeper counted as a player?

She didn't even have the same color jersey as the rest of the team.

That first season was a bit rocky. The officials kept putting colorful cards in front of my face. They insisted that I shouldn't yell at them like I did in football and basketball. I didn't think that a game in which a coach couldn't yell at a referee was much of a game. My first soccer team won 8 games, lost none, and tied 2, in spite of me. I coached varsity soccer for six years and, having learned to appreciate the game, was thrilled when my son wanted to play. Now my family joins the rest of Conyers at the RYSA fields every Saturday. The first time my son scored a goal I couldn't have been more proud if he had hit a grand slam in the seventh game of the World Series. So much for my kid never playing soccer.

Case in point number two. Dance Team. From the time my daughter was born I insisted she would never be a cheerleader or dancer or drill teamer or baton twirler or anything else than dressed up in shiny costumes and performed on the sidelines. I coached girls' basketball forever, and while I have never had anything against cheerleaders or dancers or the like—I was determined that my child would never be one. Like every other girls' coach, I secretly dreamed she would become an All-State player, average thirty points a game, and win at least one State Championship for her old man.

About a month ago, my seventh grade daughter, who has never shown an interest in playing basketball, broke the news to me that she was trying out for the school dance team. My worst nightmare was becoming a reality!

Edwards Middle School has an outstanding dance team. They preform at all of our school's football and basketball games and their coach, Donna McCullough, keeps her charges in line better than the toughest drill sergeant. She makes them work hard and keeps them out of trouble. Her program is such a success that over a hundred girls try out each spring for the 18 spots available. Dance team is a big deal, but I wasn't sure it was the right big deal for my daughter.

First I was afraid she'd make the dance team and then I was afraid she wouldn't. For weeks I went to sleep each night with the sound of music seeping through the walls and the floor jarring above me as my once little girl worked on learning intricate dance steps far into the night. During the week of tryouts the tension in our house was thick enough to cut. The most offhanded remark caused anxious eyes to fill with tears. By Friday, the actual day the squad would be selected, the entire family's nerves were on edge.

Tryouts were a three hour ordeal after school. Each girl had to dance a routine in front of a panel of judges. Some were asked to come back and dance a second time. Then everyone was sent home to wait for the phone to ring. A call from Mrs. McCullough meant that you had earned a spot on the squad and thus a chance to attend summer camp, purchase an expensive uniform and accessories, and practice ten hours a week throughout the rest of this millennium and well into the next. And I'd never seen my daughter work so hard or want something so badly in her life.

Thirty minutes after arriving home from tryouts—an eternity in middle school years—the phone rang. At least it tried to. My daughter picked it up before the ring actually escaped. I heard the scream, signifying that she had indeed made the squad. Immediately the tears started flowing. Tears of joy and thanksgiving. And when I went in to give Jamie a congratulatory hug, I noticed that her eyes were a little misty, too.

Huckaby Menagerie Gets a New Edition

It's 2006 now and Ally McCat disappeared long ago. Miss Kitty, aka Shortlife, is 17 years old, and still going strong.

There is a new baby in the Huckaby family. No, not a human baby. There hasn't been an especially bright star in the east, has there?

Our new addition is a four-legged creature. We have a

baby kitten.

That may not seem so remarkable, but you must understand--I am not an animal person. At all. In the least. I never had pets as a child and have always been uncomfortable around cats and scared to death of dogs. I didn't even like going to the zoo as a child, to see Willie B. When my wife, Lisa, and I got married, I was adamant that there would be no pets in our house. I should have made her sign a prenuptial agreement to that effect.

My no-pet rule lasted longer than I thought it would, actually. About seven years into our marriage, Lisa came home from work with a kitten. I insisted that she take it back where it came from. She asked me how I felt about separate bedrooms. I decided having a kitten wouldn't be so bad. I was wrong.

Having a kitten was worse than having a baby. There was no way to control it. It made noise all night and was always underfoot. If it wasn't, then evidence of it was. I nicknamed our kitten Shortlife, because that's what I predicted it would have around our house. I threatened to give it away and tried to get my friend, David Hays, to put it in a bag and toss it in the river.

When we'd had Shortlife about three weeks we were getting ready to go away for a weekend. Shortlife, or Miss Kitty, as the rest of the family called her, decided to pick that morning to climb her first tree--a rather tall oak beside our back deck. My family decided that we couldn't go out of town and leave the kitten in the tree, and no amount of coaxing would get her to come down, nor would saucers of milk or offerings of cat food. I tried to convince Lisa and the kids that the cat would come down on her own. After all, I've never seen a cat skeleton in a tree.

It was no use. I had to climb the oak tree and "rescue" the cat. Of course, every time I got close to her she would climb higher. There I was, risking life and limb, 40 feet high in an oak tree, trying to get my hands on a cat that didn't want to come out of the tree in the first place. When I finally caught her, she showed her appreciation by scratching my arms to pieces.

That was 10 years ago. Shortlife is still with us, and we have reached an understanding. Whenever she wants in, I let her in. Whenever she wants out, I let her out. I feed her when she's hungry and give her water when she's thirsty. Otherwise I leave her alone, and she does as she pleases. She sleeps wherever and whenever she chooses. I should have such a life.

In addition to Shortlife, we have a pen full of rabbits with names like Georgia and Dixie and Savannah. They belong to my daughter, Jamie. She takes care of the rabbits. I don't bother them, and they don't bother me. At least they have nice Southern names. Who says children can't be brainwashed.

We had a dog for a while. His name was Midnight. He was a big, playful Lab. Purebred. He was as black as midnight, thus the name. Honesty compels me to admit that I came to love Midnight. I've never known such a loving creature as that dog. We were blessed with his presence on our farm for two years and saw him grow from a tiny puppy to a giant of an animal. He roamed the fields and pastures and swam in the lake. Occasionally he went visiting around the neighborhood, but the good people at the pound always called us to come and get him - for a fee. Midnight was like folks. He disappeared on Thanksgiving weekend two years ago, along with eight other large purebred dogs from our neighborhood. What a coincidence. We may get another dog when we get over the heartbreak of losing Midnight. Another 10 or 20 years might do it.

But now we have a baby kitten. A tiny, scrawny, black little thing with white boots and inquisitive eyes. My wife and daughter conspired against me. They told me they were going to the store to get something for me and came home with a new pet. They didn't lie. They did go to the store, to buy food for me to feed the kitten.

What's a guy to do? Miss Kitty, aka Shortlife, doesn't seem to mind, so why should I? The new kitten's name is Ally, after Ally McBeal. Ally Cat. Cute.

I tell you one thing, though. I'm too old and fat to climb trees anymore. If Ally Cat climbs up in the oak tree, she's on her own.

Yeah, right. I've said that before.

It could be worse. None of my kids have mentioned wanting a pet boa constrictor. Not yet, anyway. I'll keep you posted.

Time Flies When You're Having Fun

Jamie Leigh Huckaby arrived, finally, on October 3, 1985, weighing in at 10 pounds and 3 ounces. Now she is 21 years old--and no father has ever been more proud of a daughter.

Y'all will have to excuse me if I act a bit strange for the next few weeks. I had a very traumatic experience last weekend and it has really effected me. I went to bed last Saturday feeling perfectly normal. When I awakened last Sunday, October 3, I realized that at around 12:30 that afternoon my daughter, Jamie Leigh Huckaby, would be 14 years old.

14. A one and a four. A ten and four ones. Two times seven. Almost a decade and a half. 365 days away from being eligible to drive a car, for goodness sake. How in the world could that possibly be?

It was just last week that my wife, Lisa, told me we were expecting our first child. I was a young guy with a much flatter stomach, a lot of hair on my head and none on my face. I was thrilled to learn that I would be a father. I just assumed our first child would be a boy and began making all sorts of plans for his arrival.

Those of you who are parents remember all the activity that surrounds the announcement that a new addition to the family is on the way. The first thing we had to do was remodel our small ranch house. We had to make room for more stuff. We enlisted my father-in-law, who can build anything, to build a storage house at the back of our lot so we could move some of our stuff outside in order to make room for the new baby's stuff. Didn't help. We still needed more room and enclosed the garage. Raise you're hand if you've been there and done that.

About six or seven months into our pregnancy we had something called a sonogram done. I thought a sonogram had something to do with submarines, but they did it right there in the doctor's office. He assured us that our new baby would, indeed, be a boy. I believe my reaction to this news was very typical. I sent Lisa home to paint the nursery blue while I went shopping. I bought an electric train, a basketball, a football, two baseballs, a bat, a glove, an autographed poster of Mickey Mantle, a 1985 boxed set of Topps baseball cards and a pair of Converse All Stars. Got to make sure kids get off to a good start.

When I got home from my shopping spree, Lisa was eating a hot fudge sundae, with taco chips and salsa. She sent me back out—for Varsity onion rings. She told me to hurry because I had to come home and paint the nursery blue.

The last two months of the pregnancy were a flurry of activity. Lisa spent her time cross stitching neat things for the nursery wall, which by now was blue, with rocking horse wall paper. Most of her decorations had Jamison, the name we'd picked out for our son, sewn into them.

Our first baby did not come on time. Do they ever? We looked for our new arrival throughout the month of September. This was back in the old days, when only doctors and drug dealers were allowed to carry things like beepers and cell phones, so I had to stay near a phone at all times. This created a huge dilemma when Georgia played Alabama in the football season opener.

Lisa was very understanding about my desire to see the game. She gave me a choice. I could go to the game, or I could continue to live. David Hays, who had been best man at our wedding three years earlier, stayed home and watched with me on television. Talk about a friend! We were both miffed when we didn't have to dash to the hospital during halftime. We were more miffed when Alabama won the game.

After a month of waiting and several false alarms, we checked into the hospital to have labor induced. I wasn't sure what that meant. I found out that it meant I got to sit in a chair and watch television for 26 hours while Lisa breathed funny, sweated, and screamed a lot. After more than a day of all that, some nurse came in and gave me a yellow paper gown and a white mask and made me scrub my hands with yucky red stuff. They wheeled Lisa into the operating room and I got to watch them deliver our first child by Caesarean section. I did fine, too. I didn't faint or barf—until later.

The baby was big, and wrinkled, and messy, and to everyone's surprise—a girl!

I knew we should have had that test done in a submarine.

As soon as I knew everyone was OK, I ran out and bought a pink shirt for myself, some pink roses for my wife, and a Mary Lou Retton outfit for my daughter.

We left the nursery blue, but I don't think it had a bad affect on Jamie. She has been the joy of my life and has turned into a very typical teenaged girl. We may have to have the telephone surgically removed from her ear, but other that that, she's pretty much a keeper.

If the next 14 years fly by as quickly as the last 14, next week's column will be about my grandchildren—graduating from high school.

'For Better or For Worse'—She Wasn't Just Funnin'

I'm sure Lisa Potts didn't know what she was in for when she said "I do." We've been married 24 years now--with never a dull moment.

Today is my anniversary. Well, it's not just mine. I share it with my wife, Lisa. On this very day, also a Saturday, seventeen years ago, I stood at the alter at Rockdale Baptist Church, nervously waiting for my bride to walk down the aisle and join me. The cotton farmer who was serving as my best man gave me two-to-one odds that she would be a no show. If she had known what was in store for her, she might have made a prophet of him.

Our marriage went very smoothly for the first ninety minutes. Then the honeymoon started. We had, I guess you could say, a Charles Dickens honeymoon. "It was the best of times, it was the worst of times."

We decided to honeymoon in New Orleans, because Scarlett and Rhett had. We departed the church at about 9 PM in our midnight blue Chevrolet Monte Carlo. I wanted to take the T-tops off. Lisa, then, as now, the pragmatic partner in our marriage, pointed out that the temperature was in the thirties. I left them on and we drove west.

Our first stop was at a 7-11 in Auburn, Alabama. Lisa had contracted a cold during the week leading up to our wedding and sent me in to buy Tylenol. The foreign guy behind the counter looked out at our car with "Just Married" emblazoned on the back windshield, looked down at the Tylenol on the counter, and sadly shook his head.

"Headache, already," he said with a thick accent. "Not a good thing."

I could "Amen" that.

Round about midnight we reached our destination for the evening—Montgomery, Alabama. It ain't exactly Maui, but it suited us. We checked into the nicest hotel in town, the Holiday Inn. When the guy at the front desk found out we were on our honeymoon, he gave us the George Wallace suite, complete with complimentary cigars. Lisa wouldn't smoke hers.

We checked in and Lisa went into the powder room to do whatever brides do in the powder room on their wedding night. I did what men do while brides are in the powder room—I turned on the television and found a football game.

A commercial came on. Bear Bryant, Alabama's legendary football coach, was sitting beside a table, staring at an old black and white photo. A phone was on the table beside him. Bear looked into the camera and mumbled, "Have you called your mama lately?" He paused for a moment and then added, "I sure wish I could call mine."

When Lisa came out of the powder room I had a heck of a time explaining why I was on the phone with my mother.

New Orleans was wonderful. For several days we enjoyed breakfast on our balcony, strolled through the French Quarter, took in the night clubs and fancy restaurants, rode a riverboat on the Mississippi River, and did all the other things honeymooners do. (Lisa's headache cleared up. Unfortunately, they still return intermittently.)

On the fourth night of our stay in the "City that C.A.R.E. forgot" I started getting a stomach ache. I assumed it had something to do with the 48 raw oysters I had consumed at the Acme Oyster Bar on Bourbon Street that afternoon. We tried to go about our business, but I spent the entire night in pain. The next morning, while Lisa toured the Louisiana Superdome, I toured the Superdome bathrooms. After our visit to the Dome, we took in the horse races. I was literally prostrate with pain by now, but it was Lisa's first trip to the track and she was winning. She told me to hurt in silence so she could concentrate on her race card.

To make a long story short, five o'clock found my 21 year old bride of five days weaving her way in and out of rush hour traffic, trying to find a hospital so that she could avoid becoming a 21 year old widow. She finally made it to the emergency room of the Hotel Dieu, which was not a hotel at all, but a very fine hospital.

The doctors there said that I had a bowel obstruction and needed immediate surgery. I refused. It was the day before Christmas Eve and I wasn't spending our first Christmas in a New Orleans hospital.

Lisa lied to the hospital staff and told them she was a registered nurse. It was just a little lie. She was a nursing student, six months away from graduation. The doctors shot me full of morphine, bumped two poor souls off a flight to Atlanta, and sent us home.

Within hours of landing in Atlanta I had been operated on by Rockdale's finest. We spent the rest of our honeymoon, Christmas, and New Years in the hospital. Lisa slept on a cot at the foot of the bed. I knew then that I had a keeper.

And indeed I do. For seventeen years I've been way more trouble than I'm worth, but my bride has always stayed beside me, just like she did on our ill fated honeymoon. When she said, "For better or for worse," she meant it, and I thank God for that. I couldn't exist without her.

Thanks, my love, and Happy Anniversary.

1999—It's Been a Very Good Year

*As time continues to fly by, the years seem to get shorter
and shorter. Pretty soon, January will be followed by
December and everything else will simply run together.
It's good to pause for reflection. 1999 was in some ways
the best of times, but in other ways, well . . .*

They tell me there are three days left in the Millennium. I'm not sure I believe that. After all, in two thousand years I bet somebody lost track of a day or two here and there. Don't look for a recap of the millennium here. The most talented writers couldn't recount all the great events of a thousand years in the space I'm allocated, so I won't even try.

Are we really leaving the 20th Century behind at midnight on Friday? Was the first year of this century 1900 or 1901? Technically, aren't we about a year away from the 21st century? I know you can't tell it by all the lists the magazines and television shows are coming out with. I don't agree with most of them.

Until that discrepancy is cleared up, I'm not writing an end of the century column, either. I also don't feel compelled to say good-bye to the '90s, even though I'm pretty sure we counted those days right. It's hard for me to get excited about a decade during most of which Bill Clinton was President.

Still, it doesn't seem right to end my first year as a columnist without some sort of nostalgic look back, so if you'll bear with me, I'll make note of some of my personal highlights from 1999, which was a pretty good year for the Huckaby clan.

We were blessed to be able to do a lot of traveling this year, which is one of my passions. We visited over twenty states, spent close to fifty days on the road, and made memories that will last a lifetime—and beyond. Some were as simple as relaxing under the stars in a hot tub on a mountain side overlooking Gatlinburg. That won't make my wife's list. She doesn't think outdoor hot tubs and twenty degree temperatures go together, but the other three kids in our family and I thought it was great.

I'll also never forget the thrill of being able to teach forty eighth grade history students about the Battle of Lexington and Concord by staging a giant snowball fight on the Lexington Village Green. I'll treasure the memory of jumping on a bike and, along with my kids, riding around Jekyll Island every evening "chasing the sundown." If you haven't seen the sun set over the Marshes of Glynn County in Coastal Georgia, you've missed some of God's most magnificent handiwork.

We were fortunate enough this year to spend a week on one of South Carolina's beaches. I could ride the waves of the Atlantic Ocean all day, everyday, without becoming bored, and there are enough great seafood restaurants along the Grand Strand to visit a different one every night for a year.

We spent one of the longest days of my life driving our van from Fayetteville, NC to Portsmouth, NH. I don't recommend it, but if were necessary in order to see the majesty of the Maine Coast, eat fresh lobster from roadside stands, and watch whales dive out of the blue north Atlantic and slowly submerge, waving their great tails at our boat as they disappeared beneath the surface, I'd do it again tomorrow.

I took my ten year old boy to the Baseball Hall of Fame in Cooperstown, NY, and I don't care what the women in the crowd thought about the tears in my eyes as I reached up and touched the plaques of legends like Ty Cobb, Lou Gehrig, and Mickey Mantle. The thousands of men in the place all understood.

We rode the Maid of the Mist right up to the the very edge

of Niagara Falls and saw the spectacular beauty of the Horseshoe Falls from the Canadian side. One night later we discovered that John Denver was right when he claimed that West Virginia was almost heaven. We also had the opportunity to enjoy the beauty of our own state, from the pristine Blue Ridge Mountains to the cobblestone streets of Savannah.

As great as our experiences on the road were, my best memories during 1999 didn't involve traveling. They involved people. I have had the opportunity to enjoy working with some of the best kids and most dedicated educators in the world, at Edwards Middle School and Heritage High School. As always, I've learned much more than those I have tried to teach.

I've also had the opportunity to read my very own column in this newspaper twice a week, which is truly a dream come true and I've had the opportunity to meet hundreds of wonderful people and make many new friends. Even the sadness of having to say good-bye to one of the dearest people in my life was tempered by the graciousness of friends and family.

I don't think 2000 can top 1999 for me. 1999 was truly a great year, but no matter what that little bug does Friday at midnight, I think my resolution for the new year, the new decade, the new century, and the new millennium, will be to continue to see as much of the world as I can, and to treat other people as well as they have treated me this year.

Happy New Year.

Friday Nights are Frightful When Spent in the ER

Jackson Lee Huckaby is a skinny little boy who needs to take a few assatall pills, which are special pills for those people who have no assa'tal. As often as he visits the Emergency Room, pretty soon he'll qualify for a frequent faller discount.

OK. In the words of the immortal Larry Munson, "Get the picture." It was last Friday afternoon. It wasn't the thirteenth, but it should have been. Fridays, as you know, are sacred. Last Friday was particularly precious because my basketball team had been eliminated from the region tournament the previous Tuesday and for the first time in three months I was looking forward to having a Friday evening off.

All day long I allowed myself to dream of a nice quiet evening, relaxing in front of the television. I was certain that my wife, Lisa, would be waiting for me when I got home with my slippers and a light snack to tide me over until the delicious dinner she would prepare was ready. For the past twelve Fridays our evening meal had been super sized and served with fries. I couldn't wait to get home.

It was not to be.

I knew something was amiss when I pulled into the driveway and my son, Jackson, didn't run out to greet me, demanding that we feed the cows, play basketball, rent a movie, and all the other things ten year old boys want to do when their daddies come home. Instead, I found Jackson sitting in the easy chair that I had been coveting. There was a frown on his face, tears in his eyes, and an icebag on his arm. I knew immediately that it was broken.

It was the third time Jackson has broken his arm. At least this time he had done it at school so I wouldn't get accused of child abuse like I had the other two times. Jackson, you see, is skinny. He's a skin-and-bones kind of kid who has to dance around in the shower to get wet. He doesn't have a lot of padding on his bones and when he falls on them, they break.

Jackson suffered his first broken arm one Thanksgiving. We had seen the movie "Aladdin" the day before. Jackson had been impressed with the flying carpet and was certain that if he sat on a rug on his top bunk and had his sister, Jamie, push him off, he would fly, too.

He was only four.

The mishap occurred right in the middle of the Auburn-Alabama game. The score was tied and I had Bama and the points.

Lisa was at work at the hospital and I called her and told her to meet me in the ER when the game was over. She was completely unreasonable and made me come right then. I couldn't even wait until half time.

Jackson's second fracture came a couple of years later. Of course it happened, again, while Lisa was at work and I was watching the kids. This one was the baby sitter's fault. She had let them watch "Live Atlanta Wrestling" the previous night while Lisa and I were at prayer meeting. This time his baby sister, Jenna, put him in an airplane spin and threw him off the bed. (I told you Jackson's skinny.) His wrist didn't have a chance. When he hit the floor it snapped like a green twig.

They really gave me the third degree at the Emergency Room. They were convinced I was manhandling my son. They sat me in a straight chair and aimed a flashlight in my face for hours, but I never wavered from my story. Luckily the kids told the same one.

As soon as I looked at my boy's arm last Friday I knew there would be no quiet evening at home. We were headed to the emergency room. If you've ever been to an emergency room—any emergency room—on a Friday night, you know they are anything but relaxing.

One Friday evening, while I was living in exile in south Georgia, I began having sharp pains, from indigestion, as it turned out. At the time I was certain it was a heart attack. My friend had to carry me to the ER of a local hospital. What an experience! Death would have been preferable.

We were met at the entrance by a ward clerk that I'm sure served in Hitler's Gestapo. She left no stone unturned in her mission to discover my entire medical history, all the way back to conception, and before. She got particularly upset when she couldn't force me to admit that I knew what had killed my paternal great-grandfather who died twenty-seven years before I was born.

Even worse than the ward clerk was the head nurse, Freida Von Armtwister, who made certain that I didn't see anyone who could do me any good until she had verified that my insurance company's assets were greater than the gross national product. She also made my friend verify his coverage, just to be on the safe side and made us sign oaths of allegiance to the United States and swear that neither we nor any of our ancestors had ever plotted to overthrow the government. Confederate veterans didn't count. By the time I saw a doctor, I didn't hurt anymore.

Luckily, we didn't have quite that type of ordeal last Friday. In fact, the service was relatively speedy. We were in and out in under four hours.

For the record, the cast is blue and stays on for six weeks. I don't know what Jackson saw on television last Thursday night. He says he fell down on his own, but his cousin insists he was pushed—by a girl.

I told you, he's skinny.

Birthday Outing
Helps Span Generation Gap

More evidence that the more things change the more they
stay the same. And by the way, after a slow start, the
Globetrotters won the game.

My boy, Jackson Lee Huckaby, has a birthday today. He turns 11, which is a shame in a way because ten year old boys are just about dead solid perfect and 11 year old boys turn into middle schoolers. Ugh!

We got Jackson the same day we got a new bull, Curly. Curly was a lot less trouble, but Jackson has been a lot more fun.

I wanted to do something special for Jackson's birthday so I told him he could invite four of his buddies to go to Atlanta last Sunday to watch the Harlem Globetrotters play in the new Phillips Arena. They were all excited about the trip but they all asked the same question when invited. "Who are the Harlem Globetrotters?"

I couldn't believe my ears. Has society gotten so sophisticated that we are raising a generation of children who have never been exposed to the greatest collection of clown-athletes ever to don a pair of high cut sneakers? I told the kids they were a basketball team and let it go at that.

The group met at our house Sunday afternoon for the obligatory pizza, cake, and ice cream. I drafted my buddy, Gary, to go with us to help with crowd control and we headed off to Atlanta around 2 PM. That was, perhaps, our first mistake of the day. There was another basketball game in town Sunday, the SEC Championship, and also an auto show at the World Congress Center. To say that parking was at a premium is an understatement. We had to pay for a parking space approximately what the British paid for Manhattan Island, but we finally found one. Gary and I hurried our covey of youngsters down the windblown street and into the arena. We found our seats just as the Globetrotter's mascot came out to warm up the crowd.

I thought the same thing you did. The Globetrotters got a mascot? I guess it's a sign of the times. The mascot was an acrobatic little creature with a giant globe for a head, thus the name "Globie." After a few minutes of his antics the visiting team was introduced. To our surprise, the Trotters weren't playing the Washington Generals. This day's opposition would be provided by a group of green clad giants known as the New York Nationals. They were introduced to a polite smattering of applause and then the house lights were dimmed and anticipation grew as we waited for the stars of the day to be introduced. My mind began to wander back in time and for a few moments I was ten again, too.

I remember my first introduction to basketball as played by the Harlem Globetrotters. We were spending a rainy Sunday at home and the phone rang. It was my cousin, Buck. He was all excited about this crazy group of guys who were playing basketball and told my daddy to turn on the television. He did, and there they were, in living black and white. It took us a while to figure out that they hadn't escaped from a local funny farm, but were, in fact, incredible showmen, not to mention pretty fair country ball players. I became an instant fan and looked forward to their annual appearance on television.

You remember the Globetrotters of those days, I'm sure. Meadowlark Lemon was the undisputed "Clown Prince of Basketball." He would play gags on the official, pull an assortment of trick balls out of a bag on the sideline and make hook shot after hook shot from half court. Curly Neal was a teammate of Meadowlark. He was the greatest dribbler in the history of the world. As we sat in the darkened arena, I resigned myself to the fact that the guys we were about to watch couldn't compare with the guys of my memory.

Finally the spotlights brightened and there they were, the year 2000 version of the Harlem Globetrotters, wearing the same baggy red and white striped shorts as their predecessors. *Sweet Georgia Brown* erupted from the speaker system as they formed their famous "Magic Circle" and started passing the ball behind their back, through their legs, and around their bodies at impossible angles and at a blinding rate of speed.

For the next two hours the boys in our charge were glued to their seats, mesmerized by the action on the floor. They never once asked to go to the restroom or to get snacks. In this age of high tech entertainment and short attention spans it was heart warming to know that the same tricks and stunts that brought me so much pleasure over the years could also entertain my son's generation. I think I had as much fun watching Jackson and his pals as I did the show on the floor. They smiled and giggled and laughed out loud throughout the performance.

The behind the back passes, between the leg dribbles, and slam dunks didn't captivate as they once did. They've become pretty common place. But the tricks and stunts and constant patter played just as well in 2000 as they did in 1960. It was still funny when a player teased the referee and everyone still ducked when a player tossed a "water bucket" full of confetti into the crowd. The reigning Clown Prince, Showtime Gaffney, wasn't

Meadowlark Lemon. He lacked the great elastic face of the former and he missed all three of his half court hook shots, and there was no one who could dribble like Curly Neal, but it didn't matter. It was still a great show.

What a great day! Some things really do transcend generations. Thanks, Jackson, for showing your old man the time of his life. Happy Birthday.

Precious Memories
. . . how they do linger

Precious Memories . . .
how they do linger

Some people are born into our lives. Just as blood is thicker than water, we accept these people for what they are and love them--warts and all. We laugh and cry with them. Sometimes we fuss and fight with them and sometimes we hurt with them, but we love them--whether because of or in spite of what they are--we love them instantaneously, because they are family.

Other people sort of ease their way into our lives and become a part of us gradually, over time, until we love them like family and can't really remember a time when they weren't a part of our lives.

Unfortunately, life is fleeting. We often don't appreciate the best moments of our lives until it's too late. As people come into our lives, they also go away--sometimes suddenly and unexpectedly.

Nothing is constant. Life, by its very nature, is all about change. Today's joy will be tomorrow's memories, but thank goodness for the memories. Where would we be without the memories?

They are indeed precious and, thankfully, they do linger.

Profile in True Courage

Becky Hutchins Digby loved life as much as any person I've ever known. Her's was filled with so much pain and suffering that it would have been easy for her to have become bitter. She never did. She taught everyone she touched something about living. Those of us who knew her and loved her continue to miss her, but we also are better people for having known her.

Today's my birthday. I was born on March 10, 1952. Truman was president. For you history impaired youngsters out there, that's Harry Truman, not the guy from last summer's movie. Last week was my friend's birthday. She was 45 on March 1. This column is about Becky.

When I was very young I read a book by President John F. Kennedy called *Profiles in Courage.* He told stories about people who had overcome various obstacles in life to achieve fame and fortune and great accomplishments. One of the people he wrote about was Mickey Mantle. I forget the rest. But I do know that all of the people in President Kennedy's book were yellow livered cowards compared to my friend Becky.

I first met Becky when I was in the ninth grade. Thanks to the luck of an alphabetical seating chart I became good friends with her brother, Jimmy. I met Becky when I visited their house to spend the night. I'll never forget being in their house for the first time. I was 14 and had never seen wall to wall carpeting or an upstairs or light switches on the wall.

Jimmy and I would remain great friends throughout high school and become roommates in college. I could write a book about our exploits. In fact, I already did. Becky wasn't in it. I swear. Becky started out being Jimmy's kid sister, but the two of us became close friends as time went by. She got me through two years of French in high school when I didn't know a parlez vous from a Frances. She played a piano better than . . . well, not being very cultured, I don't know who to say—but better than anyone I ever heard.

Becky had a disease called Lupus. I don't know much about Lupus, but it's one sorry and sinister illness. During the ice storm of '73, while we were both at UGA, Becky was fighting for her life at Piedmont Hospital. She was there for months. I don't remember all the particulars and they aren't important, but I do know that several highly educated doctors indicated that there was little hope for recovery. That wouldn't be the first time Becky would prove doctors wrong. She would leave Piedmont Hospital and return to school and graduate from college.

Becky was lucky, in many ways. She had a loving mother and brother and a saint for a father. For years she went through dialysis on an almost daily basis. She suffered through the agony and disappointment of two kidney transplants that failed. But here's where the courageous part comes in. Becky never let her illness get the best of her. Never. She absolutely refused to allow the dreaded disease to curtail her zest for living. She continued to live, every day of her life.

Twelve years ago I spent the longest week of my life in the intensive care waiting room at Crawford Long Hospital, waiting for my daddy to die. He finally did, on a Saturday. When I got home, totally despondent, I pushed the message button on my answering machine and there was Becky's always cheerful voice, telling me about the new kidney transplant she had gotten that seemed to be working. Just like Becky. She brought joy and happiness to the saddest day of my life.

About eight or nine years ago Becky played the piano at an anniversary party for my wife, Lisa, and me. She seemed happier than I had ever seen her. As I walked her to her car she shared a confidence. She was seeing someone and it was serious. A few months later she married Dan. Everyone who knew Becky rejoiced in their happiness.

I only saw Becky occasionally over the past few years. You know how things go. We get busy with our own lives. But every time I did run into her, she was the same Becky. Smiling, laughing, worrying about her big brother and never complaining about her numerous health complications. She never let her health shut down her life, or dim her positive outlook.

As I said, today's my birthday. I don't think there will be a celebration. My wife's not big into those kinds of things. But, boy, was there a celebration for Becky last Saturday! It was at the Baptist Church in Covington. Becky's friend, Bill Callaway, performed on the grand piano. He's the second best pianist I've ever heard. Marshall Edwards, one of the greatest preachers I've ever heard and one of Becky's truest friends, came to speak on her behalf. He was wonderful. Beyond eloquent. Hundreds were there to show how much they loved Becky. I just hope that before she passed away last week she somehow knew how much we all loved her, because I don't think I ever got around to telling her.

Her husband, Dan, hugged my neck as we were leaving the church. Southern men hug one another's necks at funerals. Through our tears he told me, "We lost a great American girl."

You got that right, Dan. You got that right.

Yes, Conyers, There Is a Santa Claus

Bernie Bourdon lived three months after this column first appeared. He was able to return home and spend time with the people he loved. He was fully aware of what faced him and did not fear death. Fittingly, his legacy is not in the way he died, however, but in the way he lived. And make no mistake, he did live!

I know it is almost Easter and not Christmas. Give me a little credit. Nonetheless, I'm writing about Santa Claus this week. You need to know about him. Trust me.

About a hundred years ago, in the *New York Sun*, Frances Church wrote a now famous response to a little girl named Virginia who had written the newspaper asking if there really were a Santa Claus. Church, of course, answered in the affirmative, but in the answer spoke of intangible qualities such as "love, generosity, and devotion." Church went on to say that just because no one had ever seen Santa Claus didn't mean he wasn't real.

I've seen Santa Claus. He is very, very real. He has lived and worked among us here in Rockdale County for the past thirteen years. He moved here, fittingly enough, on Christmas Eve in 1986. With his jolly smile, ample belly, snow white beard, and twinkling eyes, he looks just like the jolly elf Clement Moore described in his classic poem, *The Night Before Christmas*. He doesn't go by Kris Kringle or St. Nicholas or any of those other names though. To us, he is just Bernie. Bernie Bourdon.

Most of us know Bernie, but few know about him. Bernie was an executive for a telecommunications company in Canada for thirty-seven years. (That is close to the North Pole.) He retired to Florida to live the good life in a nine room house complete with swimming pool, country club membership and all the other amenities one earns through a lifetime of hard work and professional excellence. Three years into retirement Bernie's wife died of cancer and the lives of unknown thousands would change.

Bernie left the comfort of Clearwater to come to Conyers and the Monastery of the Holy Spirit. He was determined to devote himself to God's service. After spending 60 days with the other monks, his spiritual advisor in the order urged Bernie to devote himself to doing God's work among God's people. No one ever did more.

Bernie plays Santa Claus in dozens of places every Christmas. Those of us who know him best know he's not playing. Any money he ever gets for his appearances goes to his ministries. He never sets a fee. He always says the same thing when asked about compensation. "Anything you give me is more than I had before."

For the past twelve years Bernie has completely given himself to the people of our area. Sure, he has gladdened the hearts of countless children while bouncing them on his knee and inquiring about Christmas dreams and wishes. But this Santa Claus does so much more. He used his skills to begin a nonprofit organization called Techable. His company adapts computers and fits them with keyboards that can be used by those with physical challenges that make it impossible to use a standard machine. There is never a charge for the service. Techable also adapts toys so children with physically disabilities can know the joy of play. Who but Santa Claus would think of that?

Bernie also started a Meals on Wheels ministry twelve years ago and now over one hundred people a week in Conyers, Covington, and Lithonia depend on Bernie and his volunteers to bring them a warm meal and a warmer smile. But for the past few weeks, these people have been missing out. Bernie is in an Augusta Hospital, fighting for his life. One of those routine surgeries, the kind other people have, didn't go so well. I know Bernie very well. He would really covet your prayers. His very life may depend on your prayers. If you can't pray for Santa Claus, who can you pray for? I know he would want me to ask you for your prayers. He would also ask for prayers for his son Steven, who keeps lonely vigil at his father's bedside.

Bernie will also need money. As much as he'd want me to ask for your prayers, he'd hate for me to ask you for money, but he's given all of his away. He also doesn't get help from the government because he's not a citizen. Not a citizen. That's a laugh. I don't know how you can help financially, but Jessie Walker of the Conyers Kiwanis Club does. The number's listed.

Over a hundred years ago a writer for the *New York Sun* answered in the affirmative a letter from a little girl named Virginia who had written inquiring if there was, indeed, really a Santa Claus. The writer mentioned words like love, generousity, and devotion. The Sun was describing Bernie Bourdon without knowing it. The writer also mentioned that no had ever seen Santa Claus.

Well, I have. If you've met Bernie Bourdon, so have you. May God bless him.

Unexpected Treasure Found at Cooperstown

Will Rogers never met a man he didn't like. I never met a man that didn't like Jeff Autry. He was one of a kind. I loved him with all my heart and I miss him, hard, every single day of my life.

The highway sign read, "Cooperstown—Next Exit." I could hardly believe that after 40 years of hoping, wishing, dreaming, and scheming, I was within 15 miles of the Baseball Hall of Fame.

My love affair with baseball began at an early age. My bonds of affection with our National Pastime have been strained from time to time, but never broken. The Hall of Fame has been the epitome of everything baseball, at least in my mind, since I was six years old and my daddy bought me a book full of punch out baseball cards depicting all its members.

I looked at those pictures of Ruth, Gehrig, Cobb, and the others over and over, handling the flimsy pasteboard until the edges were rounded and dog eared. I memorized the statistics on back and am more familiar with the accomplishments of the big leaguers of a bygone era than I am with today's overpaid stars.

Like most boys of my generation, I lived baseball. Mantle and Mays and Koufax are as much a part of my childhood as skinned knees and the Mickey Mouse Club. I devoured every word written about the history of the game and its great players, and every book and article I read made Cooperstown seem like the Holy Grail. I could only dream of visiting there. For a boy growing up in Porterdale, it might as well have been on Mars as in upper state New York.

But there I was, less than 15 minutes from the front door. Like a child at Christmas I watched each mile roll off the odometer, thinking we'd never get there. My family thought I had taken complete leave of my senses. There is no description for how I felt as I finally handed my ticket to the red jacketed usher and walked through the turnstile into the Mecca of baseball.

It was everything I had envisioned, and more. Life size statues of Babe Ruth and Ted Williams greeted us in the museum lobby. The great hall itself was right before me with bronze plaques honoring all the legends. I went from one to another, becoming more excited with each discovery. Joe Dimaggio. Cy Young. Honus Wagner. Stan Musial. Yogi Berra. There wasn't one for Pete Rose.

For hours we explored the exhibits. The amount of memorabilia was overwhelming. Uniforms, bats, balls, gloves. I was in baseball heaven. Then I found a giant exhibit devoted completely to Babe Ruth. In awe I stood and gazed at the great man's uniform and spikes and glove and a world of other items. Then I spotted it. It was about the size of a silver dollar. Stump's Babe Ruth medallion!

Let me tell you about Stump. His real name was Jeff Autry, but everyone called him Stump because he resembled one. People also called him the "Sausage Man" because he made his living delivering his family's Holifield Farm sausage to area restaurants and grocery stores. Jeff Autry never met a stranger or had an enemy. Not a single one of either.

I met him when I coached his son, Greg. Greg was a really small kid when he first went out for my football team and I tried my best to run him off. Impossible. Since I couldn't make him quit, I made him my quarterback. He played football and basketball for me for four years. I have never coached a greater competitor.

Over the years that Greg was in my program, his family and I adopted one another. Who can say how those things happen? All I know is that for almost twenty years Jeff Autry was the greatest friend I ever had. We enjoyed life together. He was always there to pick me up when I was down or take me down a peg when I got too full of myself. He was friend, brother, and father rolled into one. Words can't describe how close we were.

Jeff was raised in an orphanage, the Jolly Home, which

brings me to the Babe Ruth display in the Hall of Fame. Babe Ruth, of course, was also an orphan. Jeff used to tell his wife, Margaret, and me about how Babe Ruth's widow would send silver medallions to the Jolly Home for the boys there to sell on the street corners of Atlanta. We always laughed at his story and pretended not to believe him. In fact, we teased him about his Babe Ruth medallions unmercifully. Of course he couldn't produce one.

Jeff—Stump—was taken from us, suddenly and unexpectedly, six years ago. He was stricken by a heart attack in the middle of the night, on Labor Day weekend. I never got to say goodbye and I've missed him hard every day since. A dozen times a day there has been something I wanted to share with him—a story, a joke, a dream for the future. The grief passes slowly, you know.

And there I was in the Baseball Hall of Fame and right there in the Babe Ruth exhibit was one of the medallions that Jeff Autry had sold, as a boy, on the streets of Atlanta. My wife and kids already thought I was crazy for the way I was reacting to my trip to Cooperstown. Now everyone else did, too, as I stood in front of the display case laughing hysterically while huge tears rolled down my cheeks.

Jeff, if the Rockdale Citizen is circulated in heaven, I saw your medallion. It was a thing of beauty—just like you were.

Did She Ever Know That She's My Hero?

My mama died in her sleep at 4 AM on December 15, 1999, four days after this column appeared. My prayer is that she died knowing how much she was loved.

It's been a tough week. My mama's sick. Not just a little sick; the kind of sick that you don't get better from. The kind of sick where the nieces and nephews come by the hospital and the children take turns sitting in a chair in the corner of the hospital room, pretending to try and sleep, while a flood of memories runs through the brain, like a cerebral version of the old television series—*This is Your Life*.

Hospital rooms have always been depressing to me. None more so than the one I sat in the other night. The white lights from the Christmas tree outside on the lawn were visible through the window, but somehow they didn't bring much cheer.

My mother has always been my hero. What's that old song? Is it something about the wind beneath my wings? She has certainly been mine. No one has ever loved two children more than my mother has loved my sister and me. Any shortcomings we have are not her fault. The only shortcoming she might have had as a mother was loving us so much that she overindulged her children on rare occasions.

It's amazing how such a strong woman, one who worked so hard all her life, can be left so weak and defenseless, ravaged by disease, beyond the help of the great body of medical knowledge we have at our disposal.

My mother was raised by a single mother during the Great Depression. She probably had as little as anybody ever has, but I never heard her complain about what she did without while growing up. I never heard her complain about anything she didn't have as an adult either.

She worked hard in the cotton mill most of her life. She was a weaver, and was thankful for the opportunity to go to work each day and earn a better living for her family than her mother had been able to earn. She worshipped my father. No man ever had a more loyal wife.

It's funny what a person thinks about. As I sat in the darkened corner of the hospital room the other night, listening to the noises in the hall, watching the clock on the wall advance, minute by minute—visions of my childhood came to me.

I remembered my mother making cornbread in the same black pan, meal after meal, year after year. I've had her show me how dozens of times. I can use the exact ingredients and cook it the exact same amount of time at the exact temperature. Mine never tastes as good as hers. Not even close.

As I studied her wrinkled face, I could see the beautiful, clear skinned lady who used to sit in the floor and play jack stones with me and let me lick the bowl when she made cakes. I wonder if kids still want to lick the bowl. I doubt it. Pretty unsanitary, I guess.

As I looked at the gray hair framing my mother's face I suddenly thought of the permanent parties the ladies on our street used to have. They would gather at our house and give one another permanents. I swear, the smell of Tony Home Permanent permeated the hospital room.

Most of my memories of my mother revolve around some form of work, for she was never an idle person. I remember counting the minutes until the 3 o'clock whistle blew at the mill. She would get home at twelve after three. We lived close to the mill. I guess everybody in Porterdale lived close to the mill. She would always come in and we would share "a bite to eat." A tomato sandwich, in season. Maybe some fried peas with a slice of onion. Only recently did I realize that she came home from working eight hours in the mill and ate a snack because she had not had lunch at work.

At six she would have supper on the table and it was always a full meal and always delicious. After the supper dishes were done she might sit down and watch television, but not without clothes to fold or sewing in her lap.

She made sure that my homework was done. She made sure that I had enough hugs and enough switchings. She listened to me say my prayers at night and woke me up in the morning. Heaven only knows what she did in between. She laughed at my jokes, bragged on my accomplishments, and traveled across the state to watch my basketball games.

She has never quit worrying about me or my sister. The few words she's been able to speak this week have been to assure us that she's all right and not to worry about her, but to take care of what we need to do.

What we need to do. We all feel like we need to do so

much, don't we? We need to work. We need to play. We need to
be here. We need to be there. We need to do a million things.

     We need to pay more attention to the treasures in our lives,
while we still have them, because all of a sudden, your greatest
treasure is lying in a hospital room and all you can do is sit in a
chair in a corner of a dark room and watch her while the light
from the world's saddest Christmas tree shines through the window and makes shadows on the wall beside her bed.

Sorting Through a Lifetime of Memories Can be a Tough Job

*Dealing with the death of a loved one is tough in a lot of
ways. My Christian faith sustained me as I watched my
mother die because I knew she would soon be in a better
place. Going through a lifetime of memories was tough
and lonely and something I never want to repeat.*

     I drew tough duty last weekend. I'm not referring to chores
created by the winter weather. Surviving the ice storm on Sunday
was a piece of cake compared to what I went through Saturday,
which was, fittingly, a cold, gray day in its own right. That was
the day that we had to clean out my mother's house and get it
ready for a new occupant.

     My mother passed away in December. She had lived in
Porterdale for my entire life and most of her own. You accumu-
late a lot of stuff over sixty or seventy years. Children of the
Depression, my parents, like many of their generation, held on to
most of what they had. My daddy, in particular, was reluctant to
throw away something just because it was old, broken, or used
up. He used to warn us that "hard times" might come back. I
hope times never get any harder than they were Saturday as I,

along with my wife, Lisa, and my sister and her husband sorted through a collection of lifetime treasures and old junk, and tried to decide which was which.

I started in my old bedroom. I knew we were in for a long day when I opened the first dresser drawer and found it full of trivial things that had once belonged to me. There were old report cards, pictures, high school newspapers and a plethora of other memories, precious to me, but meaningless to everyone else.

There was a campaign poster promoting "Maddox Without a Runoff," which hearkened back to the "Guvnah's" unsuccessful reelection campaign in 1974. That is an election night that I will never forget. Neither will former cotton farmer, David Hays. I'm not telling what happened and I hope he's not, either.

In the same drawer there was a simulated straw skimmer from Ruby Red's Warehouse, a good time emporium in the old Underground Atlanta. The hat was a souvenir from a night on the town with my college roommate, Jimmy Hutchins, and his sister Becky, who was taken from us last March.

I also found a picture of a skinny little Boy Scout on his way to Bert Adams for his first summer camp. I got homesick just looking at the picture. My first week at camp was the loneliest of my life. I don't care if I was only twelve miles from home and with all my best friends. My mama wasn't there and that was the first time I had been separated from her. The man in the picture with me was Aubrey Barnes, Porterdale Scoutmaster for I don't know how many years. We called him Boony and never appreciated the time he spent with us until it was too late to tell him. There was another picture of Boony Barnes. He was pinning an Eagle Scout award onto a strong and clear eyed fifteen year old. What a difference four years can make.

I spent thirty minutes in one dresser drawer before Lisa, the pragmatic one in our family, took over. She sent me to another part of the house, promising to put all my precious possessions in a box and take them home to a place of honor in our attic.

I went back to the den and proceeded to go through the family desk. There were just as many treasures there. I found a

Bibb Manufacturing Company pay stub from 1963. The week John F. Kennedy was killed my mother worked 56 hours in a cotton mill and brought home 112 hard earned dollars. And I complain about what teachers make.

There was a ticket from the Georgia-Alabama game in 1946 and a World War II ration booklet with three stamps left unused. There were also a box of letters addressed to Myron Ellis, my mother's maiden name. The return address indicated that they were from Homer Huckaby, my father. I couldn't bring myself to read them. Maybe on another day.

I don't know how long I sifted through the treasures in the old desk before Lisa came in and shooed me out of that room, too. I do know that there are now a lot more boxes in our attic than there were before last Saturday.

After being exiled from the den, I joined my sister in the kitchen. My mother spent the greater part of her last twelve years on earth sitting in her kitchen, leaning on the table that had been her mother's. The television and the phone were her companions. She enjoyed baseball during the summer. She was a huge Cubs fan, because their games came on before her bedtime. She watched game shows and old movies the rest of the year.

I found my sister sitting in a chair, boxing up kitchen items to give away. She picked up a heart shaped pan that was black from use. I think it was intended to be a cake pan, but my mama made cornbread in it on special occasions. For the first time that day, I cried.

We didn't exactly finish cleaning out my mother's house last Saturday, which is a bit of a problem, because we sold it last Friday. Some things just can't be done in one day. There's always next weekend. Besides, we've packed up the love letters and the cornbread pan. The rest should be a piece of cake.

5

Life Is Not a Ball game . . . ain't that a shame?

Life is not a ball game . . .

Sports has always been a big part of my life. My earliest sports memory occurred when I was four years old. I wanted to stay under the house and dig for doodle bugs with my playmate, Linda King. My daddy made me come inside and watch a baseball game with him. I was four. I didn't understand baseball, but I remember being mad as I sat on the linoleum floor of the living room watching shadowy images on our little black and white television set.

The only thing I remember, other than the fact that my doodle bug hunt was interrupted, was my daddy screaming "He did it! He did it!" over and over and a man on the television jumping into the arms of another man, which seemed strange, even to a four year old. My daddy had the foresight to make me watch the only perfect game in World Series history.

Naturally, I didn't appreciate the significance of what I had seen until many years later, but the image of Yogi Berra jumping into Don Larson's arms has stayed in my mind across the decades, along with thousands of other indelible memories of events I have experienced, or seen in person, or through the miracle of television.

Baseball was the first sport I loved. Dizzy Dean and Pee Wee Reese brought the New York Yankees of Berra, Mickey Mantle, and Whitey Ford into our living room almost every Saturday and Sunday throughout those endless summers of my boyhood. I read every book I could get my hands on about the Bronx Bombers--Ruth, Gehrig, Dimaggio--they were like the knights of King Arthur's Round Table to me.

College football, University of Georgia style, would soon rival the Yankees for my affection and attention. Red and black blood still flows through my veins and the names of Buck Belue, Bill Stanfill, and, of course, Herschel Walker, mean as much to me as the names of Charlie Trippi and Frank Sinkwich meant to my father.

Three years after Don Larson's perfect game, a man named Ronald Bradley moved to Newton County, where I lived, and created a basketball fever in the community that would infect me, perhaps as deeply as anyone. Terry Rutledge, Tim Christian, and the other Newton County Rams were as much heroes to me as the professional players I watched on television. I grew up to become a Newton County Ram and being even a small part of that outstanding program dramatically changed my life.

Basketball helped me have the opportunity to get a college education and has opened up a world of opportunity to me over the course of my lifetime. It has helped me make a living and allowed me to meet some of the most wonderful people in the world.

My mother used to get a bit put out with me over what she saw as my obsession with sports. I remember her admonishing me over and over that "life ain't a ball game." She was right, you know. It really isn't.

Ain't that a shame?

Shirt Fits to a Tee

I freely admit that I've never been much of a pro football fan, at least not since the days of Tarkenton, Unitas, and Lombardi. When the Atlanta Falcons actually made it to the Super Bowl, I had to jump on the band wagon.

All of a sudden I just had to have one. I had resisted for weeks. The tension mounted and the bandwagon filled and I resisted jumping on board. But it was Friday morning and the Super Bowl was two days away and the whole school was decked out in Dirty Bird attire and there I was in my standard khakis and oxford button down. I couldn't stand it any longer. I persuaded a friend to go out amongst the madness and find me the perfect shirt to commemorate the historic cultural event we were about to experience.

Don't misunderstand. I'm not anti-Falcons. I took more than a passing interest in the franchise when it began. After all, the NFL was still the NFL back then. Those were the days of Johnny Unitas and Paul Hornung and Sam Huff. Joe Willie Namath was a brash upstart and Vince Lombardi was master of all he surveyed. There's no need to rehash the Falcons' dismal history. It's been done to death over the past two weeks and besides, their ineptitude really had nothing to do with my disinterest in them. The Braves were just as dismal as the Falcons for years and I spent night after night watching the Superstation, listening to Pete and Ernie. occasionally venturing down to the Stadium and hoping for the miracle that finally came.

No, it hasn't been futility that has kept me from being a Falcon fan. There's just not that much of me to go around. In the fall I give my heart and soul to the Georgia Bulldogs. I was Bulldog born and Bulldog bred and when I die I'll be Bulldog dead. There just isn't enough of me left after a Saturday afternoon in Athens to offer true allegiance to another team on Sunday. It would be almost like having two wives. Heaven knows, one's plenty. So over the years I've paid less and less attention to professional football. I've always disparaged people who become rabid fans when a team hits a hot streak and then crawls back into the woodwork when times get bad. When Georgia won the National Championship in 1980 I saw people wearing red and black that couldn't spell Dawg. And ever since the Braves went from worst to first, good seats at a baseball game have been scarcer than hen's teeth. I was determined not to become a nouveau Dirty Birder. When they beat the Vikings in overtime I was picnicking beside a river in the great Smoky Mountains—oblivious to the game or its outcome.

But last Friday, I reiterate, I could stand it no longer. I had to have a T-shirt and a good friend went out in search of one. Came back with a dandy, too! It was black with the traditional Falcon emblem. It also made reference to the Dirty Bird dance craze and had a Super Bowl XXXIII logo. A perfect collectible, which is what it has now become. I wore it twice. All day on Friday, while hope still sprang eternal, and then again on Sunday, while the Broncos brought the Atlanta faithful back to reality. Nothing to do after Sunday but add my Falcons shirt to my collection of shirts that I just had to have at the time.

I have to keep those shirts in a secret place so my wife, Lisa, won't make dust rags of my cherished memories. It was fun going through the stack of old shirts Sunday night. (Why waste time?) Right there on top was my 1980 National Championship T-shirt. It's mostly threads. I wore it slap to death. I once threatened to wear it to every game until we won another championship. Ray Goff caused me to rethink that vow.

Of course I came across a T-shirt from the Braves first trip to the World Series. It had caricatures of all the players. Whatever became of Lonnie Smith, anyway? I found a shirt I bought in Gettysburg, Pennsylvania commemorating the 125th anniversary of the great battle there. Being from Americus, Georgia perhaps Dan Reeves can take some solace in knowing that at least General Lee knows how he feels.

I was confused about the logo on one particular shirt. I couldn't figure out what the slogan meant. It said, "S A W B." Then I remembered. It was a holdover from the days when Andrew Young was mayor of Atlanta and complained that the whole state was run by "smart aleck white boys." I think he said smart "aleck." There was also a 30 year old shirt with a picture of former governor Lester Maddox riding his bicycle. Backwards of course. The words emblazoned under Lester's picture summed up my feelings toward the outcome of Sunday's game. It read, "Phooey!"

The last shirt I looked at had a picture of the late Atlanta Constitution columnist, Lewis Grizzard and his dog Catfish. I was inspired! I decided I had to know what Lewis thought about Sunday's game. I put away my T-shirt collection and called The Physic Hotline. I hooked up with a soothesayer named Madame Darla. She assured me she could put through a call to heaven— for a fee. I agreed and she got right through to St. Peter. Unfortunately, Lewis wasn't there. Seems that when he found out the Falcons were in the Super Bowl he and Catfish asked for a two week pass to go and visit Satan—and get in a little ice skating.

Dream Team Caps Dream Season

I "retired" from coaching basketball in 1992. After a six year hiatus Dr. Wayne Watts persuaded me to "come out of retirement" to coach the girls' team at Edwards Middle School. I will always be thankful to Wayne Watts for that favor. He gave me back a great part of my life.

Perfection. It's the dream of every person who has ever participated in athletics. Some admit it. Some don't. I do. I want to win every time they turn the scoreboard on. I have been a player, manager and coach in Little League, Middle School, High School, and college. I've coached over fifty high school and middle school seasons in football, basketball, soccer, softball, and track. I've had very good teams—and some not so good. My teams have won championships and played in state tournaments and traveled as far as the Big Island of Hawaii, just to play basketball. But the perfect season always eluded me.

My high school team played East Rome for the state championship in 1970 at Georgia Tech. We stayed at a hotel directly across the expressway from "The Dome" and walked over for the game. I found a ten dollar bill on the ground as we entered the building. I was sure this would be our lucky night. It wasn't. The walk back across the bridge that night was a hundred miles long.

I was a manager and trainer at the University of Georgia back in the days when everyone in the Southeastern Conference that didn't play their home games in Lexington, Kentucky thought all field goals counted three points. Football was number one in Athens. Spring football was second. Basketball was an afterthought. In our first game my freshman year we lost to Rollins College. No one on our team could even locate Rollins College. The best thing that ever happened to one of our Georgia teams was getting snowed in at a tournament in Charlotte. We got to see the Jackson Five when Michael was a small black boy.

I entered Georgia as a journalism major but switched to education so I could coach basketball. I wanted to be my high school coach. I didn't want to be like him—I wanted to be him. It took me almost twenty years, but I finally realized that no one could be him. I found coaching terribly frustrating. By most yardsticks I was a successful coach, but not by the standard I set for myself. Winning never felt as good as losing hurt. I gave up coaching basketball for five years.

Two falls ago I agreed to coach the girls' team at Edwards Middle School. I told myself there would be no pressure to win. I would just teach fundamentals, help the girls learn the game, and not worry about winning and losing. I lied. I continued to live and die with every bounce of the ball. When my team lost in the semifinals of the league championship tournament last year it felt like the world had stopped turning. I wondered why anyone would ever want to coach—especially me.

And then came this year. I realized very early that this team would be special. I had a point guard who was fast as lightning released from an August storm cloud. She handled the ball like it was extension of herself.

I had wings who could handle the ball, drive to the basket, and play string music on the nets from 15 feet. I had post players who could score and rebound and play defense. I had a long bench full of substitutes who could be ready to perform at a moments notice, and often had to do just that.

More importantly, I had a group of girls who were willing to put teamwork ahead of personal glory. They were willing to practice hard and be pushed without pouting. I had a group of girls who showed up day after day, week after week; always eager to learn from their mistakes; always willing to pay the price; always willing to strive for perfection.

This team stormed through the regular season, winning all twelve games without being seriously challenged. Their average margin of victory was 30 points. They maintained their focus through the first three rounds of our league championship tournament and arrived at the championship game against Rising Starr Middle School with a perfect 15-0 record. But Rising Starr was also 15-0 and the game was at the Rising Starr gym, in Fayetteville. We had already made that long trip twice last week and had to get up Saturday morning and do it one more time. No one could have faulted these girls if they had lost, especially me. But these girls weren't about coming close. They had set a goal of perfection and meant to obtain it. It wasn't easy. They fought to a 28-24 halftime lead and then put the home team away in the second half for a 46-31 win. 16-0. League Champions. Perfect season.

Elise, Vicki, Rachel, Courtney, Jasmine, Sandriel, Stephanie, Alison, Jennifer, Michelle, Christie, Melanie, Lauren, Tiffany, Katie, Joy and Jackson. The Dream Team. A little slice of heaven and a dream come true for an over the hill, middle aged coach. Thanks ladies. You're simply the best.

A Yellow Jacket That
Even a Bulldog Can Love

Those who know me best know it takes a special person indeed to make me praise a Yellow Jacket. Wayne Kerr qualifies. (But to hell with Tech!)

It's a week until football season. Beginning next Saturday I will join 80,000 or so of my closest friends for weekly prayer meetings in Athens, or places like Knoxville, Jacksonville, and Oxford, Mississippi. We may start a new millennium here in four months but on January 1 in Oxford, Mississippi it will still be 1968.

After spending ten or eleven weeks in warm-up games,

my Bulldogs will travel to Atlanta's North Avenue for our annual bloodletting against the Trade School. Of course I mean Georgia Tech. To all true Bulldogs, they are "The Enemy."

Now understand one thing. I didn't become a Georgia Bulldog, I was born a Bulldog. I was raised on stories about Frankie Sinkwich and Charlie Trippi and the glory days when Wally Butts, Georgia's "Little Round Man," paced the sidelines of Sanford Stadium. During my formative years Georgia Tech beat Georgia almost annually, including one stretch of seven straight years. Even after Theron Sapp broke the drought, Bobby Dodd's boys seemed to have the upper hand, until Joel Eaves hired Vince Dooley to come to Athens and restore order to the world of college football. Georgia Tech was a hated word in my household. In fact, I learned to say "To Hell With Tech" before I learned the Pledge of Allegiance.

Of course, now, the worm has turned. During the past three decades Georgia has beaten Tech on such a regular basis that the rivalry has lost a bit of its edge. Some of my Bulldog brethren actually view Florida or Tennessee as bigger rivals. But not me. I don't like Georgia Tech. I didn't like them when Lenny Snow used to hurdle the line of scrimmage and I didn't like them when scholar athlete Eddie Lee Ivory gained 300 plus yards on some frozen field somewhere. I didn't like Georgia Tech when Eddie McShan refused to play one Saturday because he got his feelings hurt and I didn't like Georgia Tech when Bill Curry accused everyone but Tech of cheating to win. I certainly didn't like Tech last year when, thanks to two horrible calls in the second half, they finally broke our winning streak.

I used to tell people that I wouldn't pull for Tech with two engines out on the team plane. I still wouldn't. I used to tell people, "I don't like Georgia Tech, or anybody that does." Then I met Wayne Kerr.

I'll tell you two things right now that you can put in the bank. One—You can't be more Georgia Tech than Wayne Kerr, Class of 1973. He was a cheerleader at Tech, for goodness sakes. He married a Tech graduate who was the daughter of a Tech graduate. He has three beautiful and brilliant daughters. One, Shana, is already a Tech freshman and will spend this fall dressed in white and gold and screaming ugly things about my Alma Mater. I'm sure the other two will soon follow. All of that, and I still like Wayne Kerr, which brings me to my second point.

It's impossible for a person, in good conscious, not to like Wayne Kerr. He's what God had in mind for Adam, back before Eve turned his head. He is a genuinely nice guy who, despite what Leo Durocher said, will never finish last. He's so gracious during football season that he almost takes the fun out of beating Tech. He actually congratulates me after every Georgia win.

For those of you who may not know, or know of Wayne, let me tell you about him. Wayne Kerr. 48 years old. A dentist. Well over six feet tall and thin as a rail. He can still wear his college cheerleader sweater, and does. He has sandy blonde hair, blonde eyebrows, a perpetual impish grin, and wears a Mickey Mouse watch so he'll remember not to take himself too seriously.

I met Dr. Kerr at my church, Ebenezer United Methodist, where he has served in a variety of leadership roles, including Lay Leader and Chairman of the Administrative Board. But he does so much more for our church than fill a spot on the duty roster. If we need someone to make a serious speech to the congregation, Wayne is our man, but he's also our man if we need someone to dress up as a Blues Brother and dance the Funky Chicken. (See above reference to Mickey Mouse watch.)

Wayne Kerr's civic service doesn't end at the church door. He is a Partner in Education with many local schools and bestows the Kerr Cup, named after his father, a long time Florida juvenile court judge, to outstanding student citizens at several schools. His list of Civic Awards and memberships is longer than five miles of bad Alabama road. The Kiwanis Club, the Jaycees, this newspaper, and a dozen other organizations have had the good sense to honor him for his contributions to society in general and Rockdale County in particular.

Perhaps his greatest contribution has been to those who are least able to express their appreciation, which is just as Wayne would have it. When his dental office was condemned because the government wanted to build a road through it, he donated the building to charity and had it moved to the northwest corner of our county. Thanks to him, and others, there is now a free clinic offering dental and medical services to people in our community who would otherwise have nowhere to turn.

I could go on and on and on, but I think I can sum up my opinion of Dr. Wayne Kerr by using an oft repeated phrase of the late Lewis Grizzard. He is truly a great American. I can give no higher praise.

But I'm going to make myself hate him for three hours on November 27.

Memory Lane Winds Through Homer Sharp Stadium

High School. What precious memories were created during that awful, scary, wonderful time. Would I really relive those four years? In a New York minute!

My wife and I took a trip Friday evening. We traveled ten miles, and twenty-five years, back in time. For the first time in forever I attended a football game at Homer Sharp Field in Covington. I think it is now called Sharp Stadium. You know how things change. But some things do stay the same.

I'm a native of Newton County and Sharp Field was a big part of my childhood, my youth, and my early adulthood. My first trips there were to watch the Newton Rams play teams like Morgan County, Henry County, and the dreaded Gainesville Red Elephants. My cousin, Jerry Bouchillon, was on the football team when I was just a toddler and we would sit in the stands on Friday nights and watch him play. That was well over forty years ago. That Latin guy was right. Time does fly. It was at Sharp Field that my cousin Buck, Jerry's older brother, taught me to stand up when the band played Dixie.

When I got a little older, my neighbor Larry King's presence on the team was enough to require my attendance at all the games. By then I was at the stage of being more interested in playing two hand touch behind the end zone than watching the game. We wadded together paper cups for a football.

One of the true highlights of my humble athletic career occurred on Sharp Field when I was in the fifth grade. I won the local Punt, Pass, and Kick Competition when Corky Ballard shanked a punt. My prize was an honest to goodness Baltimore Colts football jacket, with genuine Naugahyde sleeves. I don't know how many naugas had to die to make my jacket, but I am eternally grateful to each and every one of them. I wore that sucker year round until it wore slap out.

My only experience as an actual player on Sharp Field came in the eighth grade when I was a part of a program called the Baby Rams, a precursor to the Middle School football programs we have today. I was a very bad fullback and even worse quarterback, but was on the field enough to remember the smell of the mud, the taste of the turf, and how much an underweight thirteen year old can be hurt, physically and emotionally, when he doesn't compete well on a football field.

I didn't play football in high school, but there was never a contest played at Sharp Field without me present. Honesty compels me to admit that, though a true fan of our school's football team, I was even more a fan of the Blue Rambler Band. If I were really being honest I would go a step further and admit that I was a fan of one of the band's majorettes. Whatever, if the lights came on, I was in the stadium.

After I graduated from college I came back to Covington to teach and coach. One of my responsibilities was to coach the football team at Cousins Middle School. Thankfully, I was a much better eighth grade coach than I was an eighth grade player, and some of the happiest and most satisfying moments of my life were spent on the sidelines of Sharp Field. It was there that I learned firsthand that I could make a difference in the life of young people, and that what goes on on the football field goes way beyond blocking and tackling and scoring touchdowns. My Cousin players and I had a bond that few groups have ever known, and for one wonderful night in November we were kings of our admittedly limited domain as we defeated Fayette County 45-6 to win our league championship. Championships in football on any level had not been a Newton County staple and it seemed that the whole county came out to help us rejoice.

I also coached football at Newton High and my last game at Sharp Field was also my last visit, until Friday night. The gap, I believe, was twenty years. Some things were very different from the Sharp Field of my childhood. For one, I was now a visitor. My school, Heritage, had come to do battle with Newton County's Eastside High. In addition to the aforementioned name upgrade, the stadium's sides had been switched. What once had been the home grandstand had been relegated to the visitors, and it seemed to have shrunk considerably. The home side had been moved across the field and was absolutely huge. It sported a large and modern press box and the lighting system was much improved over the old wooden post lamps that used to illuminate the center of the field and leave the endzones in semidarkness.

There wasn't a rickety wooden grandstand in sight, the home team wore green instead of blue and white, and the band didn't play Dixie. Come to think of it, they didn't have any majorettes, either. I guess baton twirling is a lost art.

But some things were the same. The smell of mud and popcorn and hot chocolate still permeated the air. When I walked around to the home side at half time to watch the magnificent Heritage band, I saw scores of the same people I sat in Sharp Field with during high school. They were watching their children play.

On the field, nothing had changed. The cheerleaders, although a bit more athletic than those of my youth, were still pretty and cheered their hearts out for their respective teams. The coaches still paced the sidelines, exhorting their charges to do their best. The players still blocked and tackled and ran and passed and played their hearts out, as if no moment in time would be more important

than the 48 minutes of competition on this warm September night.
        You know, they may have been right. They just may have been right.

Same Loving Feeling
in a Brand New Gym

*If ever anyone deserved to have a basketball facility
named in his honor, it's Ronald Bradley. He was the best
there was at what he did--or I should say, does. As the
2006 season began, he was still going strong.*

The old gym was a big brick cube, with wooden bleachers on
either side, topped by two rows of small square windows. The
floor was solid and as polished as the most precious stone. Heaven
help you if you ever strayed upon it wearing street shoes. There
were dressing rooms downstairs, under the bleachers. They resembled dungeons, especially on the visitors side, which was il-
luminated by one bare light bulb, hanging from a cord in the center of the room. The roof leaked. Buckets were hung from the
rafters to collect the rainwater. Birds roosted in those same rafters.
        In summer the gym was hot. In winter, it was even hotter,
especially on the nights the home team played basketball. The
heater and the body heat of the three thousand fans who wedged
their way into the 1800 available seats, made the gym stifling,
especially to the opponents who had to face the Newton County
Rams on the hardwood during the 17 years Ronald Bradley
coached basketball at Newton High.
        I quit telling people about Newton County basketball long
ago, for two reasons. For one thing, people who didn't experience Ram basketball firsthand just couldn't understand. Secondly,
people didn't believe the things I was telling them. I get accused

of lying often enough when I deserve to be. I didn't like being accused of lying when I was telling the truth.

From 1958 until 1967, the Newton County Rams won 129 straight basketball games at home. I know that for a fact. I was there for most of them. No team, high school, college, or professional, ever won more. As amazing as the streak was, the sheer number of victories is not the story. The story is the reaction of the people of Newton County to "The Streak," and more specifically to the players and the coach who forged it.

Every game played at the old Newton High gym was a sellout for close to ten years. Every game. Every year. Standing room only and people turned away. When the Tuckers and the Griffins and the Hart Counties of the basketball world came to town, people would line up seven and eight hours ahead of time, just to get inside the building. Every seat would be filled and people would be standing and squatting four deep around the floor. There were times when it was hard to see the boundary lines because of the spectators. I've seen grown men stand on ladders twenty feet off the ground to look through the windows.

I was describing the crowds to a college chum one day and he asked about the fire marshal. I assured him that the fire marshal was at every game. So was the sheriff, Henry Odum, Jr., who loved every kid who ever called Newton County home, but especially loved the boys with crew cuts and blue blazers who sat in one corner of the gym, watching the girls play, awaiting their turn. Those were, you see, the Newton Rams. Never very big, nor particularly athletic, they were, year in and year out, the most disciplined and most dedicated and most fundamentally sound school boys to lace on a pair of Converse All-Stars.

You could count on two interruptions in every girls' game. The first would come when the boys in blue blazers stood up to walk to their dressing room. The roar of the crowd would become so loud that the girls' players couldn't hear the officials' whistles. When the visitors stood up to go to their dungeon to dress, the chant of "Ram Bait, Ram Bait," had the same effect.

The gym was nicknamed "Death Valley" and for good

reason. Most teams who came to Covington to play were out of contention by halftime. The few times teams got close, the intimidation of the crowd and the skill of the Ram players turned dreams of upset into bitter disappointment by the fourth quarter. When the game was well in hand, the Newton students would unroll a giant banner, proclaiming to the world that the old gym was, indeed, "Death Valley." There was always a postscript scrawled under the Death Valley sign that read "We Love Bradley."

They did, too, because Ronald Bradley, the coach and architect of the Ram dynasty, brought glory and honor to an entire county, but more importantly, he taught his students lessons far more important than how to dribble or shoot or play defense. He taught them lessons about effort, and pride, and courtesy, and respect, that would last a lifetime and help them become successful people long after their basketball days were over. I know. I was one of the people.

Sunday they dedicated a new gym in Newton County. It is beautiful and modern without a single bucket hanging from the rafters. They named the new facility the Ronald M. Bradley gymnasium, not because of the winning streak he put together or the championships he won, but because of the good solid citizens he helped to build; the doctors, lawyers, businessmen, school teachers, and all the rest. They named the building for him because he touched the people of Newton County in such a way that they will never outlive his influence.

The people, fittingly, came back, to replay the old games, hug one another's necks, and remember the way it was. As I watched the people and listened to the testimonials one thing was obvious—they still love Bradley.

Know what? So do I. So do I.

It Wasn't Supposed to End This Way

*A couple of weeks after this column appeared Laney
Harris was named First Team All-State.*

Her name is Laney Harris. I first knew her when she was
seven years old. What a great kid! I can still see her in my mind's
eye. She was tall and skinny and her hair was long and straight
and almost platinum in color. She wore a perpetual grin as she
bounced around her grandfather's car dealership. She seemed to
always have a cast on her arm.

I remember taking her to Athens to watch the Lady Dogs
play basketball. Most kids tire easily at a college game and their
attention wanders to the people in the stands, the cheerleaders, the
giant mascots, and the concession stand. Not Laney Harris. She
sat on the edge of her seat, her eyes riveted on the action for the
entire game. There was a spark in her eye. Even at seven there
was a passion for the game.

I suppose Laney Harris came by her love of the game
honestly. Her mother, Donna, was an outstanding player at Cherokee County. The ageless Ron Ely was Donna's coach. He believed that girls could and should work as hard as boys long before Congress tried to legislate such matters through Title IX.

Laney's father was an All-State player at Newton County
during the Bradley days, when Ram basketball was synonymous
with excellence throughout Georgia and beyond. He went on to
star at Truett-McConnell and North Georgia College and coached
at North Georgia and Gainesville Junior College before returning
to Covington to devote his energies to raising a family.

Laney's uncle, Stan Harris, played on the 1964 state championship team at Newton County and her cousin Trudy, Stan's
daughter, also played there. She was good enough to be invited
to travel with an All Star team to the big island of Hawaii to shoot
the rock. She could shoot it, too. I know. I was the coach.

As I said, Laney Harris came by her love of basketball

honestly and has a very good bloodline.

Laney's no longer a skinny seven year old with a cast on her arm. She has grown into a beautiful young lady. She is six feet tall and slender. Her hair is still long and still very blond. She could easily be a fashion model, gracing the cover of Mademoiselle. I believe she would prefer to be featured on Sports Illustrated. She still loves basketball and has developed into an outstanding player.

Laney grew up shooting hoops with her dad in the driveway. She first played competitively when she was seven, in a ten and under boys' league. She was the best player. Although she was also a ranked tennis player, her passion lie in the roundball game, and as she became old enough for school ball, she dropped out of competitive tennis to concentrate on her basketball skills.

As she entered the ninth grade her family moved to Loganville. For the past four years she has helped the Lady Red Devils become one of the best teams in the state. Last year she led her team to the Final Four and this year's squad was ranked number one in Georgia for most of the year.

Laney is an incredible player. She has supreme court awareness and plays tenacious defense. She is an excellent ball handler and passer and deadly shooter. She averaged over 17 points a game this year. Her high was 34. She made 9 three pointers in one game and 8 in another. Her coach, Bill Bradley, who is the son of her father's coach, Ronald Bradley, insists Laney was just as valuable off the court as on.

According to Bradley, Laney infected his other players with her love of the game. She led them on a mission, to compete for the state championship. It was because of Laney, according to him, that the players worked so willingly in the weight room and the gym during the off season. They wanted to be the best and Laney made them believe they could be.

I sat and watched Loganville's last victory of the season Friday night. Sadly, so did Laney Harris. She was sidelined, her foot in a cast from a stress fracture that got continually worse instead of better. The cast was red, to match her team's uniforms.

Although she couldn't play, Laney did everything she could to help her teammates. She walked out on crutches to help form the run through line during the introductions. She sat and fidgeted on the bench, yelling encouragement to the girls on the floor. She hobbled out to meet the team during time-outs, offering water and encouragement. At one point, when her team's lead was cut to six in the fourth quarter, she helped the cheerleaders start a chant of "Defense...Defense."

When her team won, she helped them celebrate.

Loganville will not play for the state championship this weekend. They lost on Saturday night to a stronger team. Laney Harris, again, did everything she could to help her team, and she was just as crushed as the rest when their efforts fell short. This was supposed to be their year—her year. The season wasn't supposed to end like this, nursing an injury. It was supposed to end in the winner's circle. Now she and her team and the community will have to live the rest of their days with "what if . . .?"

But after the hurt and disappointment fade, Laney and her teammates will be left with the pride of knowing that they gave everything they had to be the best that they could be. There are few that can honestly claim that. And there is lots more basketball in Laney's life. Next year she will play for Furman University.

Her foot will heal, stronger than new, and with her long blond hair, she'll look great in purple.

6

What Have We Done
to Our Young?

What Have We Done to our Young?

I guess every generation is convinced that young people are going to hell in a hand basket. I remember that when I was a little boy I used Bosco, (yes, the chocolate syrup) to paint sideburns on my face so I would look like Elvis Presley. I realize I should be embarrassed by that admission, but I'm not. Everyone remembers, of course, that he couldn't be shown on the Ed Sullivan Show from the waist down because of his "vulgar" gyrations.

I wish Ed Sullivan could have lived to see MTV. He would be done forgave Elvis. Elvis might have shook his pelvis, but he never showed it to anybody on live television.

After Elvis, came the Beatles, and then the hippies, and then the war protesters. And now, all of the children of the '60s are grown up and have teenagers of their own. Many people insist that our current generation of young people are irretrievably lost.

Those folks just haven't been around the right teenagers. Sure, society and parents who have abdicated their duties as parents have created far too many mixed up kids who are searching for attention in misguided and dangerous ways. But the large majority of teens are just normal kids, trying to fit in--just like the teens of every other generation. Others are simply golden.

Parents and teachers and all other manner of adults need to remember--Raising kids is like raising a garden. We reap what we sew. We really do.

Another American Tragedy

Columbine. We'll always remember that name.

We'd reached the end of another school day. When you teach eighth graders and you're down to the final stretch, reaching the end of another school day is cause for celebration. If you've been able to overcome raging hormones complicated by spring fever and actually taught your students something, that's a bonus.

The afternoon announcements had been made and we were waiting for the buses. I turned on the television in my room, hoping to get news of the situation in Kosovo from CNN. Just as I expected, we saw more violence. Shooting, bombing, senseless killing, random death, destruction, blood, heartache, tragedy. All the things associated with war. But the scenes being shown were not from the killing fields of eastern Europe. They were from a modern high school in Colorado, located in an upscale suburb of Denver.

Students were killing students. Young people killing other young people. Again.

It's happened several times over the past three years. One time is too many. Someone walks into a school with weapons and begins creating a horror story more terrible than anything Hollywood could imagine. More terrible because it is real. Real people die. They stay dead.

As soon as my students were dismissed Tuesday I hurried home. I couldn't wait to be with my family. Safely inside our own four walls, I stayed glued to the television, as, I'm sure, millions of others did across the land. The images I saw will never leave me.

SWAT teams were everywhere. SWAT teams and schools should never be mentioned in the same sentence. There were also helicopters and a camouflaged vehicle that looked like some sort of a tank. Yellow school buses belong at schools. Tanks don't. Let me say it again. Tanks and SWAT teams don't belong at schools.

For three hours relieved students continued to run from the building in small groups, with their hands behind their heads. Parents waited at a nearby elementary school, praying that their child would be the next one transported to safety.

Dazed students frantically searched for friends and loved ones. Some cried.

Some trembled.

All were terrified.

TV reporters interviewed several students. They were all intelligent and well spoken. They looked exactly like the students in my suburban school. That's because they are. The scene could have been played out at any local school. That's the insanity of it all. Our society has come to this because we're overly permissive and have a whole generation of parents who fear being parents. We call ourselves enlightened and ridicule people who stand-up for the values our country was built upon. Heaven forbid we tread on a child's self-esteem by disciplining them when they do wrong or forcing them to conform to standards of common decency.

Something has to change in our culture. The madness has to stop. If our children are not safe in school, they are not safe anywhere. The sad thing is, the scary thing is, the absolutely terrifying thing is: There's not one thing that anyone at that school could have done to prevent Tuesday's atrocity.

What to do? Like everyone else, I wish I knew.

I do know this. We can't just wring our hands and do nothing.

Abraham Lincoln once said something to the effect that no army in the world could, by force, so much as "take one drink from the Ohio River or make one footprint on the Blue Ridge." He went on to say that if America were to die, it would be suicide; we would fall from within. Watching Tuesday's tragedy unfold, I couldn't help but think that our pulse is weakening. I don't know if the fabric of our culture is about to completely unravel, but the gruesome scene in Colorado is enough to warn us that we need to check our seams.

And Now the Monster is Here

*In my wildest dreams I never imagined that I would ham-
mer out this column exactly one month after the one on
Columbine. I pray I never have to write about such a
subject again.*

Damn!

I know this is a family newspaper. Damn, anyway.

One month ago I wrote about the horror of watching a
school massacre in Littleton, Colorado. It was terrible. It was
tragic. It was scary. It was community just like ours. It was 1,500
miles away.

This morning it wasn't 1,500 miles way. It was here. Right
here.

We were looking forward to a great day at Edwards Middle
School. The school-wide honors program was to take place.
Hundreds of students were to be honored for outstanding achieve-
ment. They were dressed in their Sunday best, eagerly awaiting
the arrival of their mamas and daddies, shortly after lunch.

Their parents came, in droves. But they came early. They
came running. They came crying. They came in a panic. They
didn't come to see their children march to the front of the gym and
receive a certificate. They came to see them -- to hold them, to
take them home and cherish them. They came just to be sure they
were alive.

Once again, the monster that has become American society reared its ugly head. This time the monster wasn't in Colorado, or Arkansas, or any other distant place. It was here. Our
eighth grade students will attend Heritage High School next year.
Their older siblings go there now. I will teach at Heritage next
fall.

The same old story. A student- turned- gunman walks
into a school commons area at the most crowded time of day and
begins firing randomly. Once again the nation's attention is focused on a school tragedy. But this time it is different.

The children who were shot were friends and neighbors. One of them I taught in Sunday School.

The snatches of conversation and rumors and names of victims were all familiar to us.

The sobbing students who were worried about their friends and family members were in my class.

The frantic parents were flooding into my school.

They were people I live with and play with and go to church with, and they were frantic because a gunman had opened fire in our school.

I walked outside to help direct parents to their children. Helicopters were circling overhead. Helicopters were circling above our school.

Students began arriving from the high school, looking for parents and younger siblings. One young man told me he heard shots and saw smoke. Saw smoke coming out of a gun in OUR school.

The bright young students being interviewed on television were all people we know.

The president of the United States was on television expressing regret over another incident of school violence in our school.

A former student came up to me looking for a hug -- from anyone. She described how she had scrambled under a bench when the shooting started. I remember telling her and her classmates, just one year ago, all the things they would need to do to survive in high school. Scrambling under a desk to avoid gunfire was not one of the things I discussed.

I said in my Littleton column that it could happen anywhere. And now it has.

Dozens of people have asked me already this morning, "How did we come to this?"

Of course I don't know exactly how. But I do know we didn't get here overnight. We got here little by little. Little by little we have become too permissive. Little by little we have given our children too much of what they wanted and too little of what they needed. Little by little we have listened to those who would tell us that firm discipline would harm our children. Little by little we've given our children more and more things and less and less attention. We are reaping what we have sown.

What will have to happen before we decide that enough is enough?

I didn't know the answer to the problem a month ago. I don't know the answer now. But I do know we better start looking harder for the answers, because the monster isn't in Colorado anymore. It's here.

Damn!

"If You Can Read This, Thank a Teacher"

I've often said that my timing is terrible. I was a student when the teacher was always right and a teacher when the student is always right. My teachers were wonderful. They had to be to put up with me.

I love bumper stickers, although I must admit many are offensive and can't be quoted in this medium. I saw one last week that read, "Clean up the South—Put a Yankee on a bus." It was meant in good fun, I'm sure. I saw another that said, "All dirt roads lead to Clemson." I know several Clemson fans who would be deeply offended by that message, if someone were to read it to them.

Many years ago, while a student at UGA, I was driving down the narrow streets of Athens behind a vintage Volkswagen Beetle. While the car was stopped at a traffic light, I noticed a bumper sticker—"Honk if you love Jesus." It was a beautiful spring day and I was feeling particularly jovial, so I gave my horn a spirited honk. The person in the Volkswagen, a very large middle aged lady, stuck her head out of the window and screamed back at me, "Can't you see the *blankety-blank* light's red?" So much for Christian charity.

One of my favorite bumper stickers of all time is the classic: "If you can read this, thank a teacher." Since schools all around the area are starting back this week, I find that message particularly appropriate. Thank a teacher. What a novel idea. I wish I could go back and thank all of mine.

I can remember my first day of school as if it were yesterday. Well, maybe day before yesterday. It was, after all, 1958. I marched into Porterdale School wearing overalls, brogan shoes, and a black eye patch, the result of a summer accident that almost cost me my sight. My teacher was Miss Ruby Jordan and if I live to be a hundred, I'll never forget her. She took me on the most marvelous journeys, introduced me to the most remarkable people, and provided the most exciting adventures any six year old boy has ever experienced. She did all this without ever leaving her classroom. She did it through the magic of reading.

In my mind's eye I can still see Miss Jordan, sitting in her straight back chair, surrounded by little "lint heads" like me, clutching a book in her worn hands. Her arms were covered with age spots. Her hair was gray and her features were stern, but the brown eyes behind her wire rim glasses held a special twinkle. She would read to us, wonderful stories of *Mrs. Minerva and William Green Hill* and the *Tales of Uncle Remus*; columns from the Atlanta Constitution and stories from (gasp!) the *Bible*. Little by little she transferred this wonderful ability to us, her students.

She clearly loved books and taught her students, at least this one, to love and cherish books, too. She also took us on walks and taught us how to hold a baseball bat, this in the days before World Series trips for four year old T-leaguers. She wiped our noses when we had colds and scolded us when we were bad. She made us popcorn balls on special days and when my class finished first grade she postponed her retirement plans and taught an extra year so she could be our second grade teacher.

Miss Ruby Jordan didn't just teach us—she loved us, and she taught us to love learning. It's been forty years since I've seen Miss Jordan. In fact, she died many years ago. But rarely does a day go by that I don't think of her and her mannerisms and little sayings. A day never goes by that I am not touched by her influence. And, of course, she went to her final reward without my ever telling her how special she was to me. I hope she somehow knew.

I was fortunate enough to have many wonderful teachers. Betty Robertson was my fourth grade teacher. No one ever made learning more fun. Mrs. Carter Robinson was the toughest teacher I ever had. We were convinced that she knew so much about Georgia history because she had experienced most of it, but she instilled a love of history in me that made me want to share it with other generations.

Mr. J.T. McKay was among the most unorthodox teachers I ever had—and one of the most effective. I can still recite poems he encouraged me to learn several decades ago. My high school civics and PE teacher, and basketball coach, Ronald Bradley, taught me that if I reached for the stars, even if I fell short, I just might land on a cloud. He continues to inspire me to this very day.

I don't remember beans about biology, but much of what I know about listening to and caring about students was derived from my biology teacher, Lee Aldridge, aka Mrs. A. Joe Croom was probably the best teacher in the history of the world, and one of the best people. Like so many of the others, he left us without my ever telling him what an impact he had on my life.

I could go on and on. Every teacher I ever had impacted my life in some way, but I think you get the point.

School is back in session and our children are, once again, in the hands of their teachers. Those teachers aren't perfect, but they sure do try hard. Take it from a little old mill village child— They don't just touch the future, they mold it. If you were able to read this, tell one, "Thanks." You can't imagine how much it would mean to them.

Lost Kids Are a Tragedy . . .
Not a Majority

*As this book went to press, PBS was still showing this
documentary and the great majority of kids in Rockdale
County were still A-OK.*

What an absolutely magnificent autumn weekend! Cool
and crisp and dry. Recent rains have washed away some of the
smog in our air, and as I walk up my driveway each morning to
retrieve the newspaper, I can actually see stars sparkling in the
night sky. Yes, I'm an early riser.

There are so many things I'd like to write about today,
like the simple pleasure of sitting by a fire, drinking coffee, de-
vouring the Saturday morning paper word by word.

I'd like to write about the World Series which we will be
hosting for the fifth time in nine years. The Yankees are coming!
Atlanta against New York. New South against Metropolis. We
took care of their junior varsity last week. Now we have to face
the A team.

I'd like to write about the glory of college football in the
South on days just like today. Georgia will be trying to stop the
Kentucky Air Force this afternoon. I sat in the broadcast booth
with a genuine living legend at the last home game. What a story
that would make.

There are a hundreds of things I'd rather write about than
the topic that I feel compelled to discuss. I need to write about
what a national documentary called the lost children of our community. Lost children. I can't think of a tougher subject. Children shouldn't be lost.

Everyone in our community, and a great number of people
across the nation, have heard about the *Frontline* documentary
about the "Lost Children of Rockdale County." Most of us saw
portions of it between innings Tuesday. Many probably saw the
replay Thursday night. It was horrifying. It was tragic. It was

distressing. It is hard to imagine that many children in our community whose parents have no idea who they are are what they are doing.

I suspect the *Frontline* crew could go into almost any suburban community and find the same number of children who suffer from having parents who have abdicated their responsibilities as parents. We happened to be the community that suffered a syphilis epidemic, so here came the cameras.

When I was in junior high we had a lice infestation in our school and our school nurse, Annie Lee Day, had to pick through everybody's hair. Some kids had to wear salve on their head under one of their mother's stockings for a few days. I'm glad Miss Annie Day didn't live long enough to have to treat the children in the *Frontline* program.

Again I say, the program was distressing. Children shouldn't be having sex. Children shouldn't be having group sex. Children shouldn't be getting drunk and staying out at night and hanging around parking lots and smoking cigarettes. Children shouldn't have to try and find their own way in today's troubled society. They should be led firmly by parents who love them enough to set limits to their behavior and enforce those limits. But all of that is not what I feel like I need to say.

This is.

The PBS documentary gave the impression that a majority of teens in the Rockdale community were as lost and misguided as the few they so vividly portrayed. It's just not so. The program gave a few minutes of footage to kids who are pursuing wholesome activities instead of drugs and sex, but it made them look like they were outside the mainstream. They are not.

I am so sick of the media glamorizing the worst of our society. I wish, just once, I could see a network give coverage to some of the positive things teens do. Every afternoon there are thousands of teens who don't go to one another's houses to get drunk and experiment with sexual deviance.

They practice softball, for instance, until they are good enough at what they do to spend a whole weekend battling against the best teams in Georgia before losing the State Championship game in eleven innings.

They march and play music, until they are good enough at what they do to go to competition after competition and come home time after time with ratings of superior.

They stay in a teacher's room, who is giving freely of his own time, and play trivia games and seek knowledge, and learn for the simple joy of learning. Then they go off to other schools and bring home trophies for knowing more than anyone else.

They roll out mats and do cartwheels and flips and stunts that you would have had to go to the circus to see twenty years ago.

They play football and basketball and baseball and soccer; they wrestle and swim and run for the joy of running. They sing and dance and perform. They visit nursing homes and go on church mission trips. They hold down jobs and do chores at home. Sometimes they simply go home and do homework or watch television or go to the movies or talk on the phone. They are good kids. There are thousands of them

Sadly, there are children in Rockdale County who are lost, mainly because their parents didn't take the time or effort to help them map out a path. It's tragic and I feel for them. But there are a hell of a lot more kids who are not doing bad things.

I wish, just once, somebody would stick a camera in one of their faces.

Quick School Fix—Chapel Programs

This column is dedicated to the memory of Mr. Joe Croom, who is probably in heaven right now explaining to Mr. Homer Sharp that the chapel program the Key Club actually put on, on Friday, was not the one he approved on Thursday night.

Everybody and his brother seem to be concerned about

the state of the public school in today's society. People say that schools are not safe and that learning is not taking place. They usually point to standardized tests, such as the Iowa Test to back up their claims. I think that's a rather unfair gauge. Most of my students have never even been to Iowa.

President Clinton is certain that adding 100,000 new teachers, at the expense of the Federal government, will solve the problem. Bill Clinton is from Arkansas. Isn't that where Lil' Abner was from? Check the performance of the students at the Dogpatch Public Schools to see how effective Slick Willie's education programs have been.

Roy Barnes thinks that holding teachers and administrators accountable for poor test performance will whip our schools into shape. Right. We're not really trying now. If Governor Barnes wants to hold somebody accountable, he needs to convince parents that students should be sent to school with the expectation of learning and behaving themselves.

I don't claim to be as smart as the president or the governor, but I have an idea for improving schools. More chapel programs. That's right. Chapel programs.

When I was in high school, back in the dark ages, before PCs, MTV, and ITBS, we had chapel every Friday morning. It was the highlight of the week. It shortened the school day, gave us something to look forward to, and introduced us to a wide variety of cultural interests.

We filed into the auditorium right after homeroom and began our program by saying the Pledge of Allegiance. After that, someone would read a short verse from the Bible and say a prayer. We weren't aware that our First Amendment rights were being trampled upon because we were exposed to the Bible and a prayer.

After our rights had been abused by our school's failure to separate church and state, we would have a program. Sometimes students would perform, sometimes people from the community would speak, and sometimes we would have an expert come and share with us. An expert, of course, is someone who doesn't know any more about a subject than a local, but is farther away from home.

I liked it when Basil Rigney's Blue Rambler Band played for chapel. Basil Rigney was a stern taskmaster who coached the band the way Vince Lombardi coached the Green Bay Packers, with similar results. Basil Rigney would probably be arrested for child abuse today for bruising the feelings of the musicians in his charge. Back then he was teaching them music, and discipline, and doing a heck of a job at both. The Blue Rambler Band closed every performance by playing *Dixie*, giving everybody an excuse to stand and cheer, right there in the auditorium, a cardinal sin under other circumstances. We didn't know we were racists and bigots. We just liked the song.

At one chapel program a year, our school counselor, Eddie Najjar would perform a hilarious skit about getting peanut butter off the roof of your mouth. Mr. Najjar must have weighed 350 pounds, but he seemed light as a feather when he danced across the stage to do his skit. I will always remember his advice for doing well on the SAT. "Get a good night's sleep and select a good set of parents." Parents again. I don't think Eddie Najjar and Roy Barnes would have gotten along.

One year, two of our students dropped out of school and joined the army. They soon wound up in Vietnam. Every week, our principal, Mr. Homer Sharp, would read letters from these two former students in which they described the horrors of war and admitted that sitting through World History was preferable to walking through a booby trapped jungle looking for Viet Cong. Both guys, by the way, made it home and returned to school to graduate.

My favorite chapel program of all time was when Linda Faye, Atlanta's first weather girl, came to Newton County High School to talk to the student body about meteorology. Before Linda Faye, Guy Sharp was cock of the walk in Atlanta weather forecasting. Linda Faye didn't have more accurate weather forecasts than Guy, but she had much nicer legs, which she showed off by coming to our school wearing the first miniskirt I had ever seen. When she walked across that stage I was very glad that I had been made to sit on the front row because I had smuggled a piece of chewing gum into homeroom. It was Juicy Fruit. The aroma gave me away.

When I looked up and saw Linda Faye standing right above me in that miniskirt I thought I had died and gone to heaven. Future cotton farmer turned land developer, David Hays, was sitting right beside me. He looked like he had been caught between a warm front and a high pressure area.

Mr. Sharp was quick to realize that none of the boys in the auditorium were likely to learn anything about weather forecasting as long as our guest stood at the front of that stage. He politely interrupted her and escorted her down off the stage and had her present her program from floor level.

Linda Faye is exhibit A in my case for more chapel programs. I don't remember the formula for finding the area of a trapezoid and I'm not sure how many elements there are in the Periodic Table, but I'll never forget the day the weather girl came to Newton High.

Roy Barnes Barking Up the Wrong Educational Tree

The Georgia teachers helped oust Roy Barnes--putting Sonny Perdue in office. Don't even ask me how that worked out for teachers.

I see in the news that Governor Roy Barnes has a grand plan to reform education. Doesn't everyone?

Somebody always wants to revamp the way schools are run. All too often it's politicians that haven't spent time in the trenches, eight hours a day, 180 days a year. They usually have a knee jerk reaction and implement a new program that has had supposedly positive results in a study done by people who turned to educational research because they found out they couldn't teach. The problem with these programs is that we often find ourselves fixing things that aren't broken, throwing the baby out with the bath water, and any number of other cliches that shouldn't appear in a ninth grade English paper, much less this column.

I've attended school for 41 of my 47 years, as either a student or a teacher. I think I am qualified to write about schools and trends in education. I've seen some real doozies, too. When I was a student at the University of Georgia I had several education classes taught by professors who hadn't been inside a real classroom in decades.

They were big on teaching about discipline in those days. Now it's called classroom management. Our professors taught us that when we became teachers we should reward good behavior and ignore bad. They said that all acting up was caused by kids craving attention and that if they could get that attention by solving an equation or answering a question about the Bill of Rights, they wouldn't stick the pigtail of the girl in front of them in the ink well, figuratively speaking.

The problem with that theory was that it was a bunch of malarkey. It was wrong, in other words. A dude, or dudette for that matter, that wants attention and doesn't get it will not stop acting out, the dude or dudette will simply resort to more outrageous behavior. "Not going to notice me sticking the girls' pigtails in the ink well, huh? Let me see you ignore my setting her hair ribbons on fire!"

Get my drift?

Another thing wrong with the above theory is that it completely disregards the fact that some kids are just mean, and that others haven't been taught to behave at home.

There was another big movement afoot in the education world when I was getting started in the profession. "Open classrooms." No longer would we squelch the creativity and imagination of our students by confining them to desks and restraining them within four walls. For an entire year I taught science in a building that had no inside walls. As I taught I could see no less than five other classes. So could my students. It's hard enough to compete for attention with twenty-five other students. Throw five other teachers and roughly 120 students into the mix and you will soon see why that particular school built walls around their previously open classrooms.

IGE was another big educational deal when I first started teaching, back in the previous century. Individually Guided Education. Every child learns in a different way and at a different rate of speed. Armed with large packets of worksheets and other printed materials, the teacher was supposed to facilitate learning by monitoring the progress of thirty self motivated students who would all love working their way through the materials. Thirty students working on thirty different lessons at the same time? No problem. Teachers, we were told, could do the job by being energetic and motivated. Right. And I'm a midget Russian astronaut.

Don't even get me started on whole language.

Now Roy Barnes says that education in Georgia is the pits and the blame falls upon the classroom teacher and the school administration. He's going to whip us all into shape. We have to shape up or ship out! He's going to improve the quality of teaching by taking away our job security. He's going to improve morale and performance by giving brand new teachers $6000 signing bonuses while veteran teachers haven't received a pay scale increase in five years because it tops out at twenty years of service. If schools don't raise performance, which Roy Barnes equates with standardized test scores, then the state will take over the schools, or allow all the students to transfer elsewhere. All that would do is lower some other school's test scores.

I have a news flash for Roy Barnes. He's wrong.

Most teachers that I've known are competent and dedicated and try their hardest to help children learn, even when the children themselves have no motivation to do so and even when there is no support whatsoever from the parents. They work longer and harder than ever before. No politician could be more disappointed than teachers when students don't learn. Threats and intimidation are not going to turn teachers into magicians. The root of the problems in education extends far beyond the class-room. In fact, it runs all the way back to the students' homes.

Roy Barnes needs to quit bad mouthing and threatening the school teachers he has and figure out a positive way to offer them help. He might discover that they aren't as easy to replace as he thinks they'll be. Throwing money at a problem doesn't always fix it.

I think most teachers feel like me. Last spring a friend said to me, "I wouldn't do your job for a million dollars."

"Neither would I," I replied. "Neither would I."

7

**Holidays...
the best times
of our lives.**

Holidays . . .
the best times of our lives

Time. We measure it in hours and minutes, days and weeks, and months and years. We begin, and end, each year with a holiday. Pretty good plan, eh?

Holidays. The special days we set aside to remember and celebrate. Christmas, Easter, Thanksgiving, the Fourth of July-- all have their own special charm. All, of course, have become too commercial and overblown and, naturally, we have all lost the true meanings of all the holidays and none are as special as they once were--back when we were kids.

Or are they? Only time will tell. I often wonder if our childhood holidays were as idyllic as we remember them. Perhaps our minds have selectively discarded certain memories, the way we sort through junk in our closets, throwing aside some memories and tucking others away for safe keeping. Time after time we pull these treasures out of the recesses of our minds and turn them over and over, examining them and embellishing them until our memories of reality replace reality itself.

Deep thoughts to introduce such a happy chapter in this book. The last thing I want to do is make someone think--particularly on a holiday. So Merry Christmas and Happy New Year. Sit back with a cold turkey sandwich or a glass of eggnog and enjoy reliving the best days of our lives.

Indelible Memories of
Childhood Christmas

This column appeared as a feature on the front page of the Rockdale Citizen on Christmas Day in 1998. My weekly columns began the next week. Eight years later, they are still running--proving that Christmas miracles do happen.

So it's the week of Christmas and school is out. I can't help but wonder if today's young people are as glad to be out of school and as full of anticipation over Christmas as we Baby Boomers were back in the '50s. Somehow I doubt it.

I was talking about Christmas with my mother last week and the subject of money came up. My mother was quick to remind me that Christmas is not about money. As usual, Mama was absolutely right. I began thinking about the Christmases of my childhood.

I was raised in Porterdale, a child of the mill village. I have wonderful memories of Christmas and very few, if any, have anything to do with money or material things.

Instead, I remember the feelings of the season and things that money really doesn't buy. My greatest fear as a parent is that I'm not providing my children the same legacy of memories and values that my hard-working and loving parents bestowed upon me.

Christmas in Porterdale was certainly different than Christmas in Suburbia, circa 1998. For one thing, it didn't begin at Labor Day, or Halloween, or even Thanksgiving. It began on the day school let out for the holidays with a community Christmas program in the Porterdale Gymnasium, a mammoth building by the standards of that day. The entire village turned out for a program put on by the children of Porterdale School. The show was heavy on scripture, prayer and Christmas hymns. The fact that leaders in Porterdale paid no attention to Supreme Court rulings concerning prayer in school didn't seem to hurt any of us.

The highlight of Christmas was seeing the giant Porterdale Christmas tree in all its lighted splendor. It always touched the ceiling of the gym, which had to be at least 40 feet tall. Neither Rockefeller Center nor Rich's department store had anything on Porterdale. B.C. Crowell would read the Christmas story, straight from the King James version of the Bible. His voice was what Luke must have had in mind when he wrote it.

After the program the students lined up and walked down to the gym floor to receive their "Christmas Boxes" from Mr. B.B. Snow, superintendent of the Bibb Mills. The boxes were brightly colored cardboard, bigger than a shoe box. The contents never varied. There were two red apples, two oranges, and two tangerines. Also two boxes of raisins, a bag of hard candy, a giant peppermint stick, and bag of mixed nuts containing pecans, English walnuts and what I've grown to learn were Brazil nuts. We children of Porterdale lived to get that box of goodies. I could make the peppermint stick last a week.

The program would last until twilight. The air always felt the same as we left the gym to walk home, our treasure box clutched under our arm. It was clear and crisp and full of magic. The town Christmas decorations would have been turned on during the program. There were giant Christmas trees in all the parks, a family of snowmen, a choir of carolers and a life-sized nativity scene. But the main attraction, without which it wouldn't have been Christmas in Porterdale, was the star on the water tower. My kids have seen light displays at Callaway Gardens and Lake Lanier and our very own horse park. Each boasts millions of lights. But I'm absolutely certain they've never been as impressed as I was with that simple five-pointed star. It didn't blink or dance or change colors. It just sat there, towering over our village throughout the Christmas season, reminding us of another star, 2000 years earlier.

Of course we had television specials in those days, but they were not on videotape at our instant disposal and they didn't include characters like Arnold Swartz-can't-spell-his-name fighting over a motorized toy. They were strictly black and white with heroes like Bing Crosby. Santa Claus wasn't in every store or on every street corner. We wrote letters to him and made list after list after list of our dreams and wishes, taken straight from the pages of the Sears-Roebuck Catalog. Of course we understood that Santa would pick one or, in a good year, two things from the list to actually bring, but it was sure fun making the list. One year I got an electric train. I ran it around that oval track for a million hours. I still remember exactly what it sounded and smelled like. Christmas trees were an important part of Christmas at our little house. Ours was never very grand and if one bulb went out the whole tree was dark, but it was decorated with love (and lots of icicles).

The week before Christmas used to last two eternities. Now it's over in a nanosecond. But I can close my eyes and be 9 again. The magic of Christmas can carry me back to the unheated bedroom of my childhood. I can feel the weight of three or four handmade quilts and the coldness of the window pane against my nose as I would peer into the dark sky, hoping against hope to catch a glimpse of Santa and his reindeer against the star-filled night sky. I remember very few of the presents I actually received, but I hope I never lose the memory of that delicious feeling of anticipation that made Christmas Eve the most magical night of year.

My life has certainly changed. I live 8 miles and a million light years from the Porterdale of my youth. I don't think my kids are spoiled, but I don't think they'd ever get excited over a shoe box full of fruit, either. There's no Sear-Roebuck catalog anymore. I can't help but wonder if my three will one day wax nostalgic over gazing for hours at an Internet toy site. Their lives are saturated with all the glamour and glimmer of what passes for Christmas these day. I don't think it's possible to find any toy that would capture their hearts like an electric train. In fact, I bought myself--I mean, my son--one a few years back. It traveled far less than a million trips around its multilevel track system before the thrill was gone. I fear that my kids are far too sophisticated to fall asleep with their noses against a cold window pane.

So, what's the answer? How can I instill in them a sense

of the magic of Christmas? I was looking through a book the other day, and I think I found a constant. The book was written by a physician. His name was Luke. The passage was familiar and still reads the same as it did when I was 9. The miracle of Bethlehem is as significant today as it was 50 years ago--or 2,000 years ago--and will be 2,000 years from now. Peace, love, hope, and joy make Christmas memories--not money. I can make sure my kids have those things. We all can.

Merry Christmas to all--"and on earth, peace, goodwill toward men."

If Not the Dreamer, Honor the Dream

I'm not sure if we've made an ounce of progress in race relations since this column first appeared--but maybe I'm wrong.

Monday off. Cool. Who'd argue with Monday - any Monday - off?

Well, for a long time a great many people argued against this particular Monday off, because this Monday is the day we set aside to honor the memory of Dr. Martin Luther King Jr., civil rights leader, Nobel Peace Prize winner--and dreamer. You remember the arguments.

"Why have a holiday in his honor when we don't have one for other great Americans like George Washington and Abraham Lincoln?"

"He caused more harm than good! The FBI said he was subversive!"

"Just one more thing crammed down our throats!"

"They can't make me pay honor to him. I don't care what they close down."

I heard them all, and many others that were even more mean-spirited. I probably even made some of the same arguments.

I was raised, after all, in a different world and my vision was admittedly colored by the times. I lived through the turmoil of the '60s. Huntley and Brinkley brought the Selma and Montgomery race riots right into my living room. Martin Luther King Jr. wasn't widely supported in Porterdale. When Bull Conner turned fire hoses and dogs on marchers in Birmingham, most people I knew pulled for the dogs. I saw state troopers surround my high school in riot gear while the student body from my county's black high school marched in protest of school desegregation policies. I saw National Guardsmen and policemen with trained dogs patrolling the streets of Atlanta, "The City Too Busy to Hate, on the night of Dr. King's death. I lived through the days of the civil rights movement without understanding anything about it.

But since those turbulent days I've been forced to study the '60s with an objective eye, in order to teach it to a generation not yet born when that fateful event occurred in Memphis. Looking at who we were during those days is not always easy and raises hard questions. Was my generation of Southerners really raised in a world where people couldn't eat in a restaurant or drink from a water fountain or sit on a bus or in a movie theater because of their skin color? Did we really hate people we didn't even know for wanting what we all wanted? Did we really curse and spit on and even kill children because they wanted to go to school and learn and be somebody? Was that really us? Sadly and shockingly, it really was.

But one man had a dream. He dreamed of freedom and justice and equality for his people and for all people. He dreamed of a country that lived up to the promises made by our Founding Fathers in documents such as the Declaration of Independence and the Constitution. He dreamed of a country united in brotherhood, a nation of individuals working together for the common good.

And he didn't just dream. He was willing to work to make his dream a reality. He marched. He made speeches. His stirring words spoke to our collective conscience. He made it impossible for fair-minded and good people to ignore the wrongs of our society any longer. He went to jail for his dream. He subjected himself to hatred and mockery and persecution for his dream. And three decades ago he gave his life for his dream.

Now we have a Monday off, and there are still those who argue that we should not honor one man, particularly this man, in such a singular fashion. Perhaps we should and perhaps we shouldn't. But even those who just can't bring themselves to honor the man should be able to honor the dream. After all, isn't the dream of liberty, justice and equality the American dream? Absolutely. Long live the dream.

Help wanted for the Valentine Impaired

The week after this column appeared, strangers stopped me on the street to ask what I finally bought my wife for Valentine's Day. I told them I bought her an iron. I really bought diamond earrings, and I didn't have to sleep on the couch.

I need help! Valentine's Day is only four days away and I haven't a clue what sweet, thoughtful, original and - above all - romantic, gift I can give to Lisa, my wife of 16 years, mother of my children and eternal sweetheart. She already has a really nice iron and I gave her an electric can opener for Christmas. I didn't skimp either. I got the deluxe model, complete with built in knife sharpener.

Back when we were dating it was easy to pick out the perfect gift. No matter what I chose, she at least pretended that it was exactly what she wanted. Flowers, candy, dinner in a nice restaurant with candle light and soft music. In other words - the usual stuff. Early in our marriage (translation - before kids) having a romantic day together was pretty easy, too. Especially if Cupid's holiday fell on a weekend, as is the case this year. We could sleep in. I could serve breakfast in bed and perhaps draw her up a nice warm bubble bath.

Even after our first child came along we could manage to find a baby sitter and have a nice dinner and take in a movie. I did learn that a romantic comedy works best for Valentine's Day. One year I took her to see that Freddy Kruger guy and wound up sleeping on the couch - alone.

Now we have three kids. Every baby sitter in the metro area has blocked our number.

If we can't go out, I need to at least come up with a special gift. But after 16 years together, I've exhausted all ideas. She has forbidden me to send her flowers because she always gets stuck paying the bill. She doesn't like getting the candy that comes in those red, heart-shaped boxes. The kids get to it first and poke their fingers in it, looking for the right type of center. The little pieces of brown paper get scattered all over the house. What the kids don't destroy is left sitting around until it's hard as a rock. We throw it out just in time to make room for chocolate Easter bunnies.

When I was much younger (and much dumber) I thought lingerie was the perfect Valentine's gift. After all, it came in red and was lacy and frilly - and *I* liked it. A few years ago I realized that all the lingerie I brought home either wound up in a box in the attic (next to my discarded T-shirts) or was taken back to the store and exchanged for something long and warm in a really nice flannel.

One year I decided that it was truly the thought that counts and made my wife a really special handmade card. I cut out the hearts myself. I sacrificed, too. I had waited until the last minute and couldn't find any red construction paper around the house, so I actually cut up one of my vintage Georgia Bulldog Schedule Calendars. She didn't seem to appreciate the significance of that gesture. I wrote a nice poem to go on the card.

"Roses are red, concrete is gray.

I love you, on Valentine's Day."

At first she laughed and seemed impressed. Then she

started looking around for the real gift. When she realized that my handmade card was it, her whole demeanor changed. The couch was especially uncomfortable that year.

I've tried taking her away on trips, too. One year I rented a nice little cabin in the mountains. How was I to know that there was a Hare Krishna convention booked there the same weekend? At least we collected a lot of flowers and reading material and the tambourines died out about 3 a.m. The next time I book a cabin I'm making sure it has a couch. That floor was hard. Cold, too!

I considered jewelry but decided against. I'm afraid I'm a little taste impaired when it comes to picking out jewelry. An old high school girlfriend once accused me of putting the tack in tacky. Besides, jewelry stores make me nervous. I went into one once. Next thing I knew I was dressed in a tuxedo, standing in front of a Baptist preacher in a church so full of flowers that it smelled like a funeral home.

As you can see, I'm in a real dilemma here and would appreciate any suggestions that you think will keep me off the couch this weekend. And just in case I flub up again - Lisa, if you read this column... no matter what inappropriate present I come up with, please know I love you. I will always love you.

Hallmark Can't Quite Say It

This column was the last Mother's Day present I was ever able to give my mother. Call your mama. I wish I could call mine.

It was my wedding night. One week before Christmas. The early part of the bowl season. Georgia vs. Penn State in the Sugar Bowl was coming up, but on this night Auburn was playing some nondescript team in the Bluebonnet Bowl. We were on our way to New Orleans for our honeymoon and stopped to spend our first night as husband and wife in Montgomery, AL. Yeah, I know.

Lisa, my bride, was in the powder room of the honeymoon suite (Yes, there was a hotel in Montgomery, with a honeymoon suite) doing whatever it is brides do to get ready to come to bed on their wedding nights. I did what grooms do on their wedding nights while brides are getting ready. I turned on the television to watch a few minutes of the football game.

A commercial was playing. Isn't there always? Bear Bryant, the legendary Alabama football coach, was in the commercial. Bear Bryant is the only football coach in America to have an animal named after him.

His face looked like it was carved out of granite. He was sitting in a chair, gazing at a black and white photograph. On the table beside the picture was a rotary telephone. After a few moments the Bear's gaze lifted from the picture and he stared right into that Montgomery hotel room The camera zoomed in on coach Bryant's face and there was a tear in the corner of his eye. Then he spoke, and his voice sounded like he had a throat full of gravel. He said, "Have you called your mama lately?" I felt like he was talking directly to me. Then he looked back down at the photograph for few more seconds and mumbled, "I sure wish I could call mine."

That had to be one of the great commercials in television history, but when Lisa came out of the powder room dressed in her lovely white satin and lace ensemble, I had a heck of a time explaining to her why I was on the phone, long-distance, talking to my mama.

Fortunately, I can still call my mama, but I don't do it often enough. Sunday is Mother's Day, the day we set aside to honor those who brought us into this world. How on earth do we do that? How can we possibly show our mothers how much we appreciate all they have done for us? No card or basket of flowers or gift could ever convey how much my mother has given me.

My mother was not a soccer mom or flower of society or business professional. She was much more. She was a mama. She worked in a cotton mill 8 hours a day then came home and cooked dinner every night. She kept our house clean, and my sister and me in clothes. She also found time to make sure our school work was done. She knew who our friends were and what we were up to.

My mother loved me enough to teach me right from wrong. She loved me enough to give me everything I needed and also loved me enough not to give me everything I wanted. She gave more hugs that switchings, but enough of the latter to keep me in line. She protected me from harm, but allowed me to try things and fail or succeed on my own. She did not meddle in my life but made sure I knew that she was, and is, always available when I need her. She did without so that I could have. She and my father made sure I knew the importance of education, and that gift has taken me places I've never dreamed of and opened doors that I never imagined would be opened to me.

Hallmark can't cover all of that in a greeting card.

Whatever way I find to try and say thank you on Sunday won't be adequate. I think what my mother would really want is what she's given me all these years.

Love. Unconditional love. As long as my mama is alive, I'll know there is one person who loves me, no matter what.

Have you called your mama lately? It think I'm fixin' to call mine.

Trick or Treat . . .
It's Goblin Time Again

My children have all outgrown Halloween. Now I have trouble getting my annual fix of candy corn, not to mention Tootsie Rolls?

Rush to the store and stock up on candy. String orange lights across your yard and rig up your boom box to play spooky music. Tape plastic witches to your front door. It's Halloween.

Halloween, has changed drastically since I was a child. What hasn't? It amazes me to ride around our community and see all the lawn ornaments and decorations that pop up before the first leaf has changed. The stores have aisles and aisles of candy, fancy decorations, and, of course, costumes. Heaven forbid a child of the nineties be forced to go out into the night and beg for candy without a designer costume and a sculptured mask.

Halloween in Porterdale had little to do with stores and spending money. Good thing. The holiday was all about kids and creativity and imagination. We got to draw Halloween pictures at school, depicting the scariest night of the year. I drew the same picture for six years, of a gray two story house with a picket fence. The fence always had a jack-o-lantern on one gate post and a black cat on the other. There were orange and yellow leaves on the trees, ghosts hovering around the house's chimney, and the silhouette of a witch flying across a full moon. Talk about imagery.

The night before Halloween was a big one at our house. My mother and I would make my all time favorite, popcorn balls. Cut-rite wax paper and Karo syrup are as much a part of my Halloween memories as the pumpkins we carved. Occasionally Mama would bake sugar cookies from dough colored with orange food coloring and my sister and I would use raisins to make faces on the cookies, which I never ate, because I hate raisins. Once or twice we made caramel apples.

I guess we weren't too worried about communicable diseases in our little school because we still did things like bob for apples. It makes me cringe to think about all those dirty little faces submerged in the same washtub full of water, trying to bite the same apples. To my knowledge, no one ever caught anything, so I guess it wasn't the worst thing in the world.

The main event, of course, was Trick-or-Treat. We children would talk about what we were going to "be" for weeks and weeks and change our minds more often than we changed underwear. We had seen store-bought costumes in the Sears-Roebuck catalog, but I can't recall anyone ever wearing one. We made our own. There were lots of hoboes wandering the streets of Porterdale on Halloween night. Just blacken your face, put on your daddy's old hat, and sew patches to your clothes. You were a hobo.

Gypsies were popular for girls. A colorful blouse, your mama's skirt, a scarf, heavy makeup and a dangly earring. Viola!

There were, of course, pirates, cowboys, witches, scarecrows, and dozens of ghosts. One of the worst whippings I ever got was when I cut eye holes in one of my mama's best sheets so that I didn't have to be a hobo for the third straight Halloween.

As soon as night fell the children of Porterdale would take over the village. We had free reign. There were over 500 houses in Porterdale and we made it a point of pride to visit every single one. There was no need for parents to accompany kids. Older siblings took care of the young ones. Every house in Porterdale was a safe house. The only thing to fear was the "Soap Sally" who might come out from under the bridge as you were crossing the river. She liked to catch little children and put them in her big black pot and make soap out of them. Luckily, I survived hundreds of trips across the Yellow River bridge without encountering her.

The treats were often homemade, which we didn't appreciate at the time. There was also bubble gum, hard candy, candy corn, suckers, and a few miniature candy bars. On one Halloween, a family on Elm Street invited everyone to come in and watch the first color television set in Porterdale for five minutes. It was better than a popcorn ball.

Children actually knocked on doors in those days and asked, "Trick or treat?" as I question. The only trick we were allowed to do was scatter acorns across the porch of the person who stiffed us on candy, and heaven help us if we forgot to thank our benefactor for a treat, even if it was an apple dropped carelessly into our bag, smashing our homemade cookies.

While we fashioned our own costumes from materials on hand, we did get to buy an occasional mask at the dime store. They were stiff pieces of plastic with an elastic band which always broke. We called them "door faces." One year, about a week after Halloween, a lady from our church, infamous for being the homeliest person in three counties, came for a visit. My sister, Myron, walked into the living room where my mother was chatting with our guest and asked, "Mama, when is she going to take her door face off?"

I'm not sure how my sister survived that incident, but she did.

Sadly, our kids can't be allowed on the streets alone, and it would destroy their self esteem if we had them make their own costumes. Heaven forbid they walk into someone's house and watch television as a treat. But, hopefully, they will make some fond memories of their own this weekend to share with another generation who just won't understand how it was in the "good ol' days."

Happy Halloween and safe trick-or-treating. But watch out for Soap Sally. She may still be out there somewhere.

Taking Time Out To Count a Long List of Blessings

God continues to bless me and my family far beyond what we could ever deserve. The fact that you're reading this book is proof positive of that. Praise God from whom, indeed, all blessings do flow.

Thanksgiving. What a wonderful holiday and what a wonderful concept--pausing to give thanks.

My thanksgiving memories are of a warm and cozy home, the Macy's parade with giant balloons, the Radio City Music Hall Rockettes, and, of course, Santa Claus. I don't remember ever sitting around the table with a multigenerational family while my father carved a turkey, ala Norman Rockwell. My mother thought turkey was too dry and was more partial to chicken, but her dressing was unsurpassed and I loved to smell the sage and black pepper in it, before she put it in the oven

My favorite part of Thanksgiving was, and still is, reading Furman Bisher's column in the Atlanta Journal-Constitution every year. We were a Constitution family and Bisher writes for the Journal, but the issues were always combined for the holidays. I hope Mr. Bisher won't mind, but I am going to be bold enough to share some of the things I'm thankful for this year. They say that imitation is the most sincere form of flattery. Consider yourself flattered, Furman.

I'm thankful, for one thing, that my family had the newspaper delivered to our doorstep every morning, even when we had little else, and I'm thankful that we had the Encyclopedia Britannica and other books, even when we had to go outside to find our bathroom. Reading changed my life.

While I'm being thankful for my childhood, I'll go ahead and say that I'm thankful for being raised in Porterdale, during a time when entire towns really did help raise children, and for the Bibb, who provided more than everything we needed.

I'm thankful that I don't still have to go out on the back porch to use the bathroom, but also thankful that I am isolated enough from my neighbors that I can if I want to.   I'm thankful my wife doesn't edit my column, or my last blessing wouldn't have been counted, at least not in this public forum.

I'm thankful for young people who say "sir" and for signs on restaurant doors that say "Thank you for not smoking."

I'm thankful that Larry Munson tells me about the Georgia games I can't see in person, and I hope he lives forever, because Georgia football wouldn't be the same without him. While we're on sports, I, for one, am thankful for the thrills the Braves have given us in the '90s, because I remember all too well the '60s, '70s, and '80s.

I'm thankful that I don't live in Buffalo, or Pittsburgh, either, for that matter, and I'm thankful that an entire continent separates me from California.

I'm thankful that my sister and brother-in-law are spending this Thanksgiving in a brand new home.

I'm thankful for stadium seating in theaters, because no matter how tall the person in front of me is, I can still see.

I'm thankful for the onions in Waffle House Hashbrowns,

the butter, salt and pepper in grits, and Tabasco and shredded cheese in chili. I'm thankful for fried catfish, any time, anywhere, but especially at Clarence Henderson's on a Saturday night. I'm thankful for the person behind the counter at the Varsity that will still scream at me, "What'll ya have?" instead of saying, "May I help you?" I'm also thankful that more restaurants seem to be willing to prepare my salad for me, instead of sending me to a bar to make my own.

I'm thankful for the headlights of my wife's car coming down the driveway in the middle of the night, after she's been called in to deliver a baby. Time and the stork wait for no man!

I'm thankful that my middle-school-aged daughter is at the school every afternoon after school, practicing with the dance team, instead of the places some children find to go. I'm also thankful that my ten year old son wants to go to the gym with me and that my second grader loves to read as much as I did. And I'm thankful for the smell of Crayola crayons.

I'm thankful when, at church, we sing a song I know by heart, if for no other reason than I don't have to put on my glasses to read the words in the hymnal. And I'm thankful when the speaker, any speaker, says, "In conclusion . . ." (especially if he or she means it.)

I'm thankful for long walks in the woods and that I live in a place where an inch of snow can create a 24 hour holiday.

I'm thankful for the doctors and nurses at Newton General Hospital who have taken such good care of my mama this week, and although I won't get to eat her dressing tomorrow, I'm thankful for the previous 47 Thanksgivings in which I did.

I'm especially thankful that the little lady from Montezuma has given me the privilege of sharing my thoughts, opinions, and general foolishness with the readers of this newspaper for the past eleven months, and hope I can to continue for a long, long time. And I'm thankful for the readers who tell me how much they enjoy my column, even when it's not as good as it should be.

Happy Thanksgiving, and may God bless you all.

'Tis the Season to Shop 'til You Drop

A wonderful thing happened shortly after this column appeared. Someone stole my wife's credit card. I let them keep it. They spend way less than she does.

It became official, I believe, as soon as the funny looking guy with the beard hit the high note Thursday night and the Rich's Christmas tree exploded into light. The Christmas shopping season is here. Beware of women searching for gifts!

Yesterday, of course, was the biggest shopping day of the year. Stores opened before the sun even thought about coming up and offered all sorts of enticements to draw customers. One department store chain offered color televisions at about a third of their normal price. The ad said limit of two. Most people thought that meant two per customer. They really meant two per store. Sure, the chain lost money on each set they sold, but they made up for it by selling chocolate covered cherries and Grill-o-matics at huge markups. It's a great country, isn't it? All kinds of ways to make money—all you have to do is figure out what they are.

My wife and teenage daughter like to sleep. It's their passion. 364 days a year I have to hire the Third Army Band to wake them up. OK. So, I really use a tape of the Third Army Band. You get the point. They are bad about wanting to sleep all day. But not the day after Thanksgiving! They are up before dawn and ready to shop until they drop. Literally.

They had plotted all day on Thursday with the other female members of the family. While we men were sitting around the living room, belching, watching football on television, and eating one more piece of pecan pie, the women turned the kitchen into a war room. Maps of the metro area were taped to the wall with malls, shopping centers, and free standing stores highlighted with color coded markers. Ads from the morning newspaper, which had to be brought in with a wheel barrow, by the way, were spread out all over the table and counters. The place looked like

Eisenhower's bunker on the eve of D-Day.

This massive planning strategy began shortly after lunch at one family member's home and continued through turkey sandwiches and more dessert at a second person's house. Finally, the battle plans were laid. The lists were compiled, the check books and charge cards were inspected and pronounced ready, and the cell phones, vital for communication about unannounced sales, were charged and ready to go. An eerie silence fell over our house as the females in my family put out their clothes for easy access and went to bed.

Now I know what you're thinking. You're thinking, "What does this male chauvinist pig know about shopping? He probably walks into a mall, goes directly to what he wants, buys it, and leaves the store."

You're exactly right. But I do know what I'm talking about when I describe shopping on the day after Thanksgiving. I once accompanied my mother on such a trip. We went to Belvedere Mall and every car in Atlanta was there. Those of you who are natives to the area will know how long ago that was. The rest of you will have no knowledge of anyone having ever shopped at Belvedere Mall. We drove around in the parking lot for over an hour before giving up and leaving. The day was not a total loss, however. We bought a pair of roller states at the hardware store on Candler Road. That reminds me. Anybody know where I can find a skate key?

I also ventured out on a shopping expedition as an adult on the morning after Thanksgiving—once! I was looking for a Cabbage Patch Doll. You remember the craze, I'm sure. I wanted to "adopt" one for my newborn daughter, a real one; one that had a cloth face and Xavier Robert's autograph on it's bottom. I stood in line at a Toys-R-Us along with several thousand females in track shoes and warm-up suits. The smell of cologne hung over the air like napalm. Finally, the junior assistant store manager approached the front door carrying a big ring of keys. He wore a frightened look, like a deer caught in headlights. When he swung the door open the women stampeded. I'm not sure what happened to the door opener. One moment he was there and the next he was gone. I hope he didn't leave small children behind.

I didn't get a Cabbage Patch Doll that day, but luckily, my wife's aunt, a battle hardened veteran of dozens of one day sales, did, so Jamie didn't have to suffer through life as the only child in her generation to have to grow up without a doll with an autographed butt.

Yesterday seemed to go well for Lisa and Jamie. I was a bit concerned, I must admit, when American Express sent a complimentary limo to drive them to the mall, but when they returned late last night they looked content and the garage held most of what they bought. Besides, they explained, "Christmas only comes once a year."

Thank goodness for that.

And in case you're wondering, my Christmas shopping is already done, too. I'm giving everyone on my list cookbooks called "Dinner on the Grounds." If you haven't gotten yours, there are only 27 shopping days left until Christmas.

O' Christmas Tree, O' Christmas Tree

In case you're wondering, this year's tree was the best yet.
But, then again, aren't they all?

This weekend will be the biggest of the year for the purchase of Christmas trees, which has become a giant industry in this country. What hasn't?

Christmas trees have always held a special place in my heart. Nothing is more magical than a Christmas tree, with sparkling lights, brightly colored ornaments, and tinsel.

When I was a child my daddy always bought our family Christmas tree at the local Big Apple. The truth be known, my daddy didn't believe in spending more than one or two of his hard earned dollars on a tree that would be tossed in a few days, so most of our trees were of the Charlie Brown variety. Still, decorating that tree was one of the highlights of the year. We only had a couple of strands of lights and they were the kind that if one went out they all went out. By most standards, our trees were pretty barren, but not to us. My mama always said, "It will look just fine when we get the icicles on," and it always did.

Ideals Magazine changed my opinion of Christmas trees. Ideals was a beautiful magazine, full of beautiful pictures, stories, and poems. In fact, a local lady, Mrs. Mamie Ozburn Odum, often contributed her poetry to the publication. The *Ideals Magazine* always had pictures of elegant Christmas trees, beautifully decorated, with hundreds of lights. I got spoiled by looking at those pictures and dreamed of having such trees.

My mother, always willing to help our dreams come true, took over the Christmas tree buying duty and would hoard her extra change to be able to afford a nicer tree at Christmas. The only thing she ever hid from my father was how much she paid for our Christmas trees.

We were traditionalists. We used multicolored lights that didn't twinkle, even when white lights became the rage. We never went to the small bulbs and never used bubble lights or any of the other fads. Mama always put the lights on the tree, then we would get to help hang the ornaments, including a very special string of little glass beads, shaped like Christmas bells. The icicles went on last and we had a constant battle as to whether they should be hung separately and delicately or tossed in the air and allowed to fall where they would. Families have broken up because of the great icicle debate.

During the '60s someone came up with an aluminum Christmas tree. If you remember where you were when JFK was killed, you remember aluminum Christmas trees. You didn't put lights on them, just glass balls, all of the same color. My sister had to have one. The ornaments on ours were red, but the Christmas my brother-in-law was in Vietnam we changed to blue. We had a big color wheel to shine on the tree, which would change from red, to blue, to green, to orange, as the wheel rotated. We set the aluminum tree up in the front room and kept our real tree in the living room.

I never got over my love affair with Christmas trees and when Lisa and I were married, I vowed to have the biggest Christmas tree our dwelling would hold, regardless of costs. The first year of our marriage we began a tradition that has lasted 17 years. All year, we empty our pockets of change, every day, into a big jar. On Thanksgiving night we wrap and count our coins and use the money to buy our tree and new decorations. You'd be amazed at how the money adds up each year and we don't have to feel guilty about spending too much for our tree.

Of course we buy a real tree. I'd move to New Jersey before I'd put up an artificial tree. We usually drive to the State Farmer's Market to choose our tree. People buy houses with less time and effort.

I usually lose my religion, not to mention the Christmas spirit, when we get the tree home and I have to get the tree to stand up straight. I wish one of those NASA rocket scientists would do something really useful, like design a Christmas tree stand.

I send everyone out of the house for several hours while I put the lights—multicolored, of course, on the tree. Last year there were 2000. *Ideals Magazine* doesn't have anything on me anymore. Putting two thousand lights on a twelve foot tree can be very frustrating and sometimes I say words little kids shouldn't hear.

After the lights are in place and my family returns from exile, we eat supper—boiled shrimp and oyster stew—and then we trim the tree with the hundreds of ornaments we've collected over the years. Some are homemade and some are Hallmark's best, but all have a special place in our heart, and on our tree.

We've had our share of Christmas tree disasters through the years. We can tell the same stories as everyone else—of every needle falling off and trees having to be replaced on Christmas Eve—of trees crashing to the floor in the middle of the night—of lights going out all at once—but when I see the magic in the eyes of my children as they sit in front of the fire and stare at our tree, night after night, I believe that all the trouble we go through in our quest for the perfect tree is worth it, and I have yet another blessing to count.

By the way, I'm putting the lights on our tree tomorrow afternoon. If you're anywhere in the vicinity of Ebenezer Road— cover your ears.

"This is a Christmas to Remember"

This column was written and submitted to the Rockdale Citizen by my daughter, Jamie, as a Christmas surprise for me. It was one of the best Christmas presents ever.

> *"Setting our hopes on a big snow tonight*
>
> *We'll wake up to a world of white,*
> *It's gonna be a Christmas to remember.*
> *Light up the fire with Nat King Cole,*
> *Always sentimental and don't you know that*
> *It's gonna be a Christmas to remember."*

The chorus of Amy Grant's "A Christmas to Remember" just about sums it all up. Think back. Go ahead--it's not that hard. Go back in your mind to all the Christmases in the past. Christmases filled with holly, trees, carols, and Santa Claus.

Maybe you remember when the Rich's tree was still on top of the Rich's bridge and maybe you used to ride the "Pink Pig". Remember the Christmases when you used to buy cute little Richie bears that wore sweaters and hats.

If you think back really hard you may even remember a Christmas when it snowed. You might remember when aluminum Christmas trees and big colorful lights were the decor of most houses in America or when Jimmy Carter thought that if we didn't use Christmas lights we could conserve energy.

When you were little, did you go to Christmas Eve services at church and then maybe even go look at all the Christmas lights? You probably couldn't sleep at night because you were so excited about what you might find under your tree the next morning--and heaven forbid--you might have even peeked--trying to get at least a glimpse of Jolly Old Saint Nick. I've been told that Santa used to only make wooden toys. Maybe your best memories are trying to find the perfect gift for your parents and loved ones.

Those are great memories that we all have and you probably have your own collection of memories to add to my list. But a lot has changed. We still fill the holidays with wreaths, carols, trees, cookies, and Santa. Rich's still has a giant tree--but it's no longer on top of the bridge. It still lights up on the high note of "O Holy Night." The pink pig no longer exists and I know few people who even remember ever riding it--all who haven't are very deprived. Richie Bear is no longer wearing a cute little sweater with Christmas trees but this year he's wearing a tux with "2000" written on it. I wouldn't call it cute, either. The clerk asked me if I would like to buy one but I told her that I would prefer Macy's adorable Millennium Snoopy. And have you noticed that most things aren't focused on Christmas this year as much as the New Year?

I don't even remember the last time it snowed. I've never seen an aluminum tree--well, take that back--I think that's what Lucy wanted on *It's Christmas Charlie Brown!* Now we cover our houses with white icicle lights. And we don't even give a thought to saving electricity. Santa must not even know the meaning of wooden toys--now children's gifts are video and computer games.

ChristmasEve services are still held and people still drive around just to look at Christmas lights. Children can't sleep on Christmas Eve and never will, and Santa better be careful at night, because we still peek. And we still look for the perfect presents for those we love so much. Daddy --this is for you.

But let's concentrate on THIS year. Let's make memories this year. I've already started. I made very bad sugar cookies. I mixed up two recipes. I guess Rachel (character on *Friends*) is not the only klutz when it comes to the kitchen.

> *"Time doesn't stand still*
> *Many things change*
> *But some things never will*
> *The memories we share*
> *The songs we always sing"*

So join me and let this Christmas truly be " A Christmas to Re-member."

Jamie Huckaby

Christmas—A Time for Sharing

Many people wrote me after this column appeared and said that it inspired them to do something extra for others during the Christmas season. What a great compliment!

Christmas is only three days away? How did it get here so fast? Remember the expression, "slow as Christmas?" It's obsolete, for me at least. I think I still have boxes in the basement from last Christmas.

Christmas is a time for memories. I'm pretty big into memories. My friends are often amazed that I remember details of our shared past that they just can't quite recall. My wife, Lisa, has a ready explanation for that. She says that I remember things that never happened.

During this time of year radio stations and newspapers and school teachers who are desperate to keep their students busy, and quiet, for a few moments solicit Christmas memories from their listeners, readers, and rowdy students, respectively. In fact, this column began on Christmas Day, one year ago, when I took time to write about my memories of Christmas in Porterdale, during my childhood.

Just last week, I was thrilled to see that my daughter, Jamie, had written an article for this paper about her Christmas memories. I was a bit apprehensive about what kind of memories I might have helped make for her. My biggest concern as a parent is that I will raise spoiled children who value the material things in life over the things that are really important.

I was very pleased as I read Jamie's piece. She wrote about the anticipation leading up to Christmas morning and of trying to stay awake to catch a peek of Santa doing his work, but didn't mention one present or gift.

Mostly, Jamie remembered the sights and sounds and feelings of Christmas. She remembered many of the same things I treasure so much. The joy of decorating the tree, the wonderful music of Christmas, the lights and decorations, and, more than anything, the feeling of peace and love and happiness that comes from having one's family and loved ones gathered together for a celebration of love.

During this time of year, however, I always feel a twinge of sadness, and perhaps guilt, because I and my family have been so blessed and because there are so many children in the world who will not have the opportunity to experience the kinds of Christmases that my children experience. I'm not referring to the Christmas morning memories when my children rub sleep from their eyes and come down the stairs to explore the myriad of gifts Santa has strewn across our living room floor. I'm talking about the other side of Christmas. The important side.

There are children in Rockdale County who have never even witnessed a church play at Christmas, much less had the opportunity to don a halo or bathrobe and play the part of an angel or a shepherd. They've never been inside a church, followed their mothers fingers along a hymnal, or heard the beautiful story from Dr. Luke's book about a baby King who was born in a stable and rested upon sweet-smelling hay in a far away manger.

There are children who are growing up without traditions of any kind. That is so sad to me. Building family traditions

doesn't have to cost.   Every Christmas Eve, just before bedtime,
I don a silly looking Santa Claus hat and my family joins me on
the hearth for the reading of "A Night Before Christmas," followed by the real Christmas story from the Bible.   There are so
many children who have never even sat down for a meal with all
of their family present.

There are many children who have never known the joy
of wishing for a special gift and then finding it under the tree or in
a brightly wrapped present on Christmas day.   That is sad.   But
it's not as sad as knowing that there are children who have never
known the joy of giving to someone else.

My very favorite Christmas memory came when I was
about seven years old. My daddy had been given the task, by his
Sunday school class, of taking "Christmas" to a family who otherwise would have none. We filled up the trunk of his old Buick
with things for the family, who lived out in the country in a small,
unpainted house.

We drove up into their yard on the afternoon of Christmas
Eve. A worn out looking lady in a faded house dress answered my
daddy's knock on the door.   Dirty faced children seemed to be
everywhere. They watched in amazement as we brought in a tiny
little tree, a string of colored lights, a few ornaments, and a box of
icicles.   The mother put her brood to work decorating the tree
while we brought in the rest of the stuff.

There was a hot meal and groceries and Bibb Christmas
boxes, which contained fruit, candy, and nuts.   There was also a
set of clothes for every child, a wrapped present for each, and a
bag of toys for the mother to distribute after the children had gone
to sleep. The children were beside themselves with excitement. I
don't know the mother's name, but even though it has been forty
years, not a Christmas goes by that I don't see her face in my
mind's eye, with tears rolling down her cheeks as she watched her
children celebrate Christmas.   I think I remember tears in my
daddy's eyes, too.

I wish the whole world could know the feeling I had that
Christmas. I'm sure there are families in our community who are

doing without this year, too. Three days left until Christmas. Maybe it's not too late to find them.

Christmas Greetings to Those at Work

This column remains dedicated to the public servants who sacrifice their time and energy for the rest of us--even when it means working on Christmas Day.

It's Christmas Day. The most special day of the year. If you have kids, as we do, you've been up since very early this morning. In fact, it might seem as if you've hardly slept at all, what with waiting up for Santa and all.

Christmas Day is, of course, a day for traditions. Maybe yours is to have a big breakfast, before opening mountains of gifts. Maybe your family gathers for a huge Christmas dinner, which is in the middle of the day, by the way. The meal in the evening is supper. Whatever your traditions, I hope you've been able, as I have, to spend your Christmas day in the comfort of a nice warm home, surrounded by people you love.

Some folks don't get to do that, you know. Some folks have to work, even on Christmas Day. I'd like to salute them. They are the people who give us Aunt Sally's phone number in Detroit when we decide we want to wish her a Merry Christmas and can't find her number to save ourselves. They are the people at the Waffle House who feed us if we have to be on the road, speaking of which, they are also the people who work at the hotels, motels, and inns across the nation. I seem to remember an innkeeper who played an important part in the first Christmas.

They are the people who work at convenience stores so that we can run out and buy batteries that didn't quite make it down the chimney and the folks who make it possible for us to rent tapes and video games, or go to a movie. I feel especially sorry for those people. I assume they aren't working by choice, but because of someone else's greed. Heaven forbid, we miss a chance to make an extra nickel, even on Christmas Day. If Ebenezer Scrooge were alive today, Bob Cratchit wouldn't even get the one day a year off.

Many people are at work right now because we just can't get along without them. For them there are no silent nights, no matter what date appears on the calendar. Take the firefighters for instance. We don't think about them unless we knock over a heater or an electric wire short circuits and we find our house ablaze.

The police officers are working, too. It would be nice if we could get the criminals to promise and take Christmas off, but anyone who has seen "Home Alone" knows that criminals just can't be trusted. Someone has to monitor the jails today and some-one has to patrol the highways. Someone has to insure our safety while we are enjoying our holiday at home.

The EMT's in our community are on duty, too. Just in case, you know. And the men and women of the Armed Forces are spending Christmas far from home, helping fulfill the long ago promise of "peace on earth."

Don't forget the doctors and nurses. Please don't forget the doctors and nurses. My wife was a nurse for fifteen years. She spent her share of Christmases away from the family cel-ebration. I'll not pretend that I was ever happy about her absences. This year she's at home, but if she weren't, I know I'd be much more understanding.

I've had the opportunity to observe doctors and nurses up close and personal over the past month. I now understand why nurses have been called angels of mercy. I knows the ones who cared for my mother throughout the seemingly endless nights would rather have been home with their families, but you would never have known it. I'm sure many of her care givers are at work right now, taking care of people who need taking care of.

My wife is now a nurse-midwife. That means she goes to the hospital and births babies. Babies don't pay much attention to

the clock or the calendar, either. They may come at any time—
night or day—even on Christmas. When the phone rings, off she
has to go, into the night. Perhaps there are doctors and midwives
delivering babies and taking care of mothers at this very instant,
while we're having another piece of pecan pie or taking a nap in
our new recliner.

Two thousand years ago there was a young couple traveling far from home. The woman was pregnant, and sometime during the night, her time came. She was probably scared to death,
being in a strange city and far from home. Someone probably
went for a midwife, who had to leave the warmth of her own home
to go out into the night to deliver a baby and take care of a new
mother—a stranger.

I'm glad she did, because we're having a pretty nice birthday celebration at our house for the child she delivered. I wonder
if the midwife's family minded that she went to work in the middle
of the night. I wonder if anybody thanked her. I wonder what
would have happened if she hadn't gone when the call went out.

I wish I could take a piece of sweet potato pie or a cup of
hot cider or some form of Christmas cheer to all the public servants who are spending Christmas Day working on our behalf. I
can't. But I can say thank you, and I will. Thank you, and if I
may paraphrase the words of Dickens's Tiny Tim, may God bless
you, every one. Merry Christmas.

Long List of "Bodacious" Resolutions

*As this book went to press I had not broken every single
resolution, but it was very close.*

Happy New Year, y'all. If you are reading this I guess it's
safe to assume that the world didn't come to an end on the stroke
of midnight. If you're reading it inside, using electric lights, then
the Y2K bug wasn't the monster it was supposed to be. If someone is having to read this to you, you're either too young to under-

stand much about this column, or you partied last night like it was 1999. Whatever the case, Happy New Year, y'all.

This is the day, of course, to make resolutions—to pledge to do things differently in the year 2000. The year 2000? It's really here, isn't it? Hard to believe. I remember sitting around with my friends in high school, talking about the dawn of the new millennium and trying to figure out if we'd still be here to see it. Sadly, some of us aren't. Things like car wrecks, cancer, and the Vietnam War kept many of my high school classmates from the big party last night.

I actually made it, and 47 isn't nearly as old as it looked in 1970 when I graduated. Funny thing. I spent New Year's eve sitting in front of the television watching Dick Clark host the countdown at Time's Square. I did the same thing 30 years ago. I got older. He didn't. But I digress. Then again, don't I always?

Resolutions. Usually I resolve not to make any because most of them are broken by the time the last college bowl game kicks off, anyway. But this year, I do have a long list of resolutions. Something about starting a new century seems to make New Year's resolutions almost mandatory. However, my resolutions won't be of the usual eat less, exercise more, spend less variety. No, indeed. If I'm going to publish a list of resolutions, I'm going whole hog. I'm going to allow myself to be a little bit bodacious.

For starters, I'm not going to promise to eat less. In fact, I'm determined to eat more. My wife and Dr. Atkins have turned me into skin and bones over the past two months. My pants are falling off and I've taken up my belt as many notches as I can, so I'm going to go back to eating more—especially catfish. I wonder if Henderson's Restaurant is open tonight? I'm going to eat more grits, too. After all, grits is groceries. And I'm going to have cornbread at least twice a week and fry chicken at home once a month. There. It's in writing! Ask me in March how this resolution is going.

I'm also going to work less and play more. I recently discovered that the world would not stop turning on its axis if I wasn't busily engaged around the clock. I'm going to make more time for my family and myself. I was recently reminded that none of us will live forever.

I also resolve to take long walks in the woods, read Uncle Remus stories to my kids, even when they are not interested in hearing them, and turn off the television, especially when it's just on for background noise. I'm going to play more board games, tell more stories, and make someone laugh, every single day.

In the year 2000 I'm going to turn back the clock and write letters to my friends—the kind with paper, pen, envelopes, and stamps. If you don't get yours soon, let me know. I'm going to smile more and worry less. I'm going to try and be a little more Southern. I've noticed lately that I've started speaking faster and have all but stopped slurring my R's. I've got to watch that.

I would resolve to clean out the basement and laundry room, but that would take until the next century and prevent me from fulfilling all my other resolutions.

I'm going to spend less time on the freeway and drive the back roads more. I'm going to forgo franchise fast food joints and eat at family owned restaurants every chance I get.

I'm going to take my boy fishing more than twice this year.

I might clean out the gutters and replant the tulip bed, but don't hold me to those.

I am, however, going to do the crossword puzzle, if not every day, at least once a week.

I'm going to try and be a little more obnoxious when it comes to college football. I've tempered my emotions a bit over the past few years. I've actually tried to be gracious toward opponents, whether Georgia wins or loses. I don't really like being that way. I'm going back to gloating over victories and being sullen when we lose.

I'm going to get all of my columns in early and actually meet the publication deadlines for all of the books I have in the works.

Above all, I'm going to give thanks for every new day,

because each day is a gift not promised us. And I'm going to try my very best to live, every day of my life, in 2000 and beyond. I hope you do, too.

Happy New Year, y'all.

Mardi Gras or Not,
New Orleans is Hot

My most eye-opening New Orleans experience occurred over 25 years ago. My buddy made me promise never to reveal his identity. So far, I haven't, but there's a chance I could be bought--cheap.

Today is just another Wednesday for most of us. We went to bed last night right on schedule and grumbled a little this morning when the alarm clock went off, but eventually crawled out of bed and stumbled to the kitchen for that first cup of coffee—the one that turns us from groggy zombies into normal human beings.

About 500 miles west of here, however, today is anything but normal. It's the day after Fat Tuesday, which is the culmination of the carnival period known as Mardi Gras.   Way down yonder in New Orleans they have been celebrating the survival of another winter with parties and parades and a general spirit of debauchery. Last night, on the eve of the Christian season of lent, was the big blowout. There ain't enough aspirin in the world to cure the headache hanging over the Crescent City today.

I've been to New Orleans on a number of occasions, the first when I was 16 and passing through with a group of Boy Scouts. Our leaders walked us through the French Quarter at 7 o'clock on a Sunday morning. Even then we saw things our tender eyes would never forget.

My wife, Lisa, and I honeymooned in New Orleans, just like Scarlett and Rhett.   We'd been on Bourbon Street for maybe five minutes when I was approached by a skinny little street urchin, who looked to be about twelve, but who was wise beyond his years. He walked right up to me and said, "Hey, mister. I bet you ten dollars I can tell you where you got your shoes."

I was thirty at the time. He was, as I said, about twelve. He was way smarter than me. I thought about his proposition for a moment and then decided to teach him a lesson. I knew he had no way of knowing that I had gotten my shoes at White's Department store in Covington, GA. I agreed to the bet. He made me promise not to squelch and then handed a ten spot to Lisa to hold. I did likewise and then asked, "OK, where did I buy my shoes?"

He grinned up at me and responded, "Hey, man! How do I know where you bought your shoes. I don't even know you. I said I could tell you where you *got* your shoes and you got your shoes on your feet, on Bourbon Street, in Orleans parish in New Orleans, Louisiana, in the US of A. Pay up!"

I'd been had, but it was ten dollars well spent. I've gotten way more than ten dollars worth of enjoyment from telling the story.

I was in New Orleans during Mardi Gras one time. It was in the late '70s and the policemen were on strike. As soon as I arrived in the city I made the same mistake thousands of others did and parked in a no parking zone on Canal Street. When I came back to my car, three hours later, there was a ticket on the windshield, along with a note explaining that while the policemen might be on strike, the members of the Louisiana National Guard were not. Another expensive lesson in the city that C.A.R.E. forgot.

I can't say that I really took part in Mardi Gras. I was more like an observer and spent most of my time standing around with my mouth open, staring in disbelief. It's amazing what alcohol can do to people's inhibitions. It's also amazing what otherwise normal and rational human beings will do for a string of plastic beads thrown from a Mardi Gras float. I won't go into the details, but if you know someone who has been to Mardi Gras and comes home with an inordinate number of beads, you can bet that person won't tell his or her mama too many details about the trip. The city claimed they were going to crack down on flashing this year. I heard they made 400 arrests. That's like filling up a mayonnaise jar with water in hopes of draining the ocean.

A college buddy and I stopped off in New Orleans on our way back from the Cotton Bowl in Dallas one year. For some inexplicable reason, we signed up for a night life tour, the kind usually reserved for blue haired ladies from Des Moines and their husbands. Sure enough, we were the only two people on the bus younger than 70, but we had a great time. One stop we made was at the 500 Club, where we saw an exotic dancer named Sandra Sexton. My friend got a much closer look at the feature attraction than I did. He was invited up on stage to be a part of the act. The dancer rewarded him afterward with a great big kiss and an autographed photo.

He was the envy of the entire bus. Retired salesmen from Toledo and Topeka slapped him on his back and congratulated him on his good fortune as we made our way to the Cafe du Monde for beignets and cafe au lait. He was so pleased with himself that he carried his souvenir picture into the restaurant.

We were laughing and talking and replaying the events of the evening. My buddy had just taken a big bite of his powdered donut and a big sip of coffee to wash it down when a waiter, noticing the picture of Sandra Sexton, said to us, "I see you've been down to the 500 Club. You know, Sandra Sexton used to be a guy."

My buddy sprayed powdered sugar and coffee all over the folks at our table. He had assisted, and kissed, New Orleans's first sex change stripper.

I don't know what kind of stories people will bring back from Mardi Gras this week, but if they can top mine, I'd sure like to hear them.

8

"There's a Sweet, Sweet Spirit in This Place . . ."

"There's a Sweet, Sweet Spirit in this Place . . ."

The Bible tells us that if we raise up a child in the ways of the Lord, he will not stray from that path when he grows older. That's not an exact quote, of course, but I believe I got the general gist of the passage right.

I was, indeed, raised up in the ways of the Lord, in the Julia A. Porter Methodist Church in Porterdale. What a great congregation of believers they were! My father taught the Gleaner Sunday school class in that church for many years. He was a student of the Bible and taught me to be, also.

I'll not claim for one moment that I have always lived according to the lessons of life I learned so well at the Methodist Church in Porterdale, but I do know that I've never fallen beyond the help of the Lord's grace, and that is a comforting thought. To paraphrase one of the old standards from the Cokesbury Hymnal, the way of the cross most certainly does lead home.

Thankfully, I've found a church home for my family and myself at the Ebenezer United Methodist Church, about a stone's throw from my mailbox. We don't use the Cokesbury Hymnal any more, but we still pay lots of attention to the red words in the scriptures--the ones Jesus spoke.

This chapter is dedicated to all the wonderful saints who helped teach this little ol' linthead boy that Jesus loves even me.

I Could Almost See the Scars

It's's easy to know what Jesus would have us do in a given situation. Actually doing it can be a whole 'nother matter.

It was July hot in August. I don't know exactly what that means, but I heard it in a song once and liked the way it sounded. Taking my wife and three small children to Washington D.C. for summer vacation sounded like a good idea when we planned the trip—in February. After five days in our nation's capitol, we had had about all the fun we could stand for one week. It was the last morning of our trip and we were eating breakfast in the Union Station Food Court.

If you haven't been to Washington, you should. It's a national treasure. Sadly, it is overrun with homeless people, con artists, and panhandlers. Sometimes it is hard to tell them apart. During our week in Washington we had heard every conceivable story known to man in an effort to pry money away from the tourists. I had become very adept at ignoring pleading eyes and outstretched hands.

Back to Union Station. My wife had secured a table amidst the throng of people. I was trying to juggle two trays laden with biscuits, eggs, hashbrowns, coffee, orange juice, and the like—typical fast food breakfast fare. A young man in a green fatigue jacket came up to me. He had long hair, a three day old beard, and carried a backpack. I made a point not to look into his eyes as he approached me and asked for a handout. I didn't even pay attention to his words. I just gave him the brush off and began to sort out my family's food items.

The young man then did a strange thing. He thanked me, even though I hadn't given him anything, including one moment's attention.

I watched him as he walked up to a well dressed man at the next table. This was obviously a businessman, on his way to work. He was dressed in an expensive looking blue suit, a briefcase was at his feet, and he was reading the paper. This time I did listen to the young man, even though he wasn't talking to me. "Might I have a bit of breakfast?" he asked the fellow at the neighboring table.

The man looked up from his paper into the youngster's dark brown eyes. Without saying a word, the businessman tore in half the Styrofoam plate that held his breakfast and raked half of it onto the portion of the tray he had torn off. He handed this to the young beggar, along with an unopened carton of milk.

The young man thanked his benefactor, carried his breakfast over to a counter, then bowed his head and said grace before he began to eat.

I felt like two cents as those words from Matthew that I learned as a child and have taught my children echoed in my brain. "That which you do for the least of my kingdom, you also do to me."

I watched the stranger with new eyes as he picked up his food and began to eat. I could almost see the nail scars in the young man's hand.

What Would Jesus Do?
Rest When He Was Tired for One Thing

I hope reading this column does for you what writing it did for me. It reminded me that God made the seventh day for rest because He knew that we all needed to, probably much more often than we do.

"In the beginning was the Word, and the Word was with God, and the Word was God. . . And the Word became flesh and dwelt among us." I didn't write that. John did. A long time ago.

Pretty neat story, huh? What a concept. God came to

earth and lived among the people. Not only did he live with us, he was one of us. The Bible tells us that while he was a man on earth Jesus *was* a man on earth. He lived with his family, ate food, drank wine, worked in his daddy's carpenter shop, went fishing with the boys, and did what people do. He knew temptation and fear, minded his mama, and even cried when his friend died.

He spent three years as an itinerate preacher. Did real well, too. It's been two thousand years and folks are still talking about his sermons. He walked all over his part of the world, never had a parsonage to call his own, cared for the sick, fed the hungry, and taught the people. Of course he had to attend numerous committee meetings with his disciples. With a schedule like that it stands to reason that Jesus, having become a man, would get tired. When he got tired, he withdrew from his work and rested. Says so right there in the Bible, in several places.

Jesus came to earth, of course, to die for our sins. I'm no theologian, but I also believe he came to show us how we should live our lives. Even Jesus rested when he was tired, and he knew that he couldn't really rest in the midst of all the hubbub and confusion he lived and worked in. Time after time scripture tells us Jesus went off alone to rest and pray, to commune with his Father.

Jesus was showing us what we should do. In today's world we move in dozens of directions at the same time. We work too much so that we can buy things and store up riches on earth. We drive our kids around at a dizzying pace, trying to keep them in every activity imaginable. The busier we are, the more we seem to take on. I'm more guilty than anybody. Sometimes we need to do what Jesus did when he got tired. We need to find a place of solitude. We need to rest. We need to talk to God. We need to listen for His reply.

My family and I did that over a recent weekend. We found a marvelous place called Covecrest Christian Retreat and Conference Center, in the north Georgia mountains. We rented a little cabin. It had a kitchen and a front porch with rocking chairs, but didn't have a television or telephone or any other electronic devise. My kids didn't know how they would survive.

They survived by fishing in the pond, walking in the creek, climbing nearby mountains, and standing under an icy cold waterfall. We even sat on the front porch and read books and pulled out a dusty Cokesbury hymnal and sang camp meeting songs.

Jesus knew what he was doing when he went off alone to rest. We should try it more often. It makes life better. I wonder how many other good examples he set for us.

Saying goodbye isn't easy . . . Even for us Methodists

As this book went to press, David Hancock was alive and well at Oak Grove UMC--still.

I've been a Methodist all my life. In fact, my mother claims I was a Methodist for nine months before I was born. The first trip I took, other than home from the Porterdale Hospital, was to the Julia A. Porter Methodist Church on the first Sunday of my life. The Cradle Roll in that church was one of the first places the name Darrell Huckaby was ever recorded. You get the picture. I am a lifetime Methodist.

The history teacher in me won't allow me to write about being a Methodist without recognizing the fact that John Wesley began the Methodist Church along the Georgia coast shortly after James Oglethorpe founded the colony. Near Christ Church on St. Simons Island stands the Wesley Oak under which Wesley is purported to have preached. It has been said that Wesley was "set on fire with the Holy Spirit and people came from miles around to watch him burn."

Shortly after Wesley's methodical manner of worship had became a new Christian denomination, itinerant preachers, called circuit riders, began to travel across Georgia and the south on horseback, spreading the gospel and ministering to backwoods populations. As Methodism grew and evolved, the idea of the itinerant preacher remained. Every Methodist preacher is an itinerant preacher. There are no permanent appointments in the Methodist Church. When a minister arrives to pastor a church, it is understood that it is just a matter of time until he or she will be leaving.

I told you that to tell you this: Having been a Methodist for 47 years, I have seen a lot of preachers come and go. All have brought great joy, some upon coming and others upon leaving. I'll never forget the preachers of my youth. One of my favorites was A.J. Bruyere. His father had played for the original Green Bay Packers the ones sponsored by the meat packing plant, and he had a scale model of Lambeau Field, complete with handcarved players, in his office. On Sundays when the Falcons were in town, you could rest assured that the sermon would be very short. Preacher Bruyere, on those Sundays, would be halfway out of his robe before the benediction was pronounced.

When I was about 12 or 13, Preacher Bruyere went on a Sabbatical to the Holy Land. His interim was Dr. Dallas Tarkenton, father of UGA and NFL legend Frank Tarkenton. Every teenaged boy in the church came every Sunday while Dr. Tarkenton was with us in hopes that his famous son would show up. One Sunday he did, and played touch football on the lawn after the service. It was the greatest day in church since Pentecost, or at least we boys thought so.

During my high school days a saint of a man named Harold Lyda was pastor at Porterdale. Preacher Lyda was tall and thin and one of the most humble and sincere people I've ever met. About the same time the Reverend Lyda was with us, Bill Cosby had out a hugely successful comedy album in which he talked about his boyhood friend, Old Weird Harold. I wish I could say that the youth of the church never used that nickname for our pastor, but I can't. I can say, however, it was never meant to be mean spirited or disrespectful. In fact, Harold Lyda had a positive impact on my life that, I fear, he'll never know about.

I have known dozens and dozens of other Methodist ministers. Some, of course, I've known better than others. Although

I've known many and respected most, I love at least one--David Hancock. David Hancock came to my church, Ebenezer United Methodist, five and a half years ago, along with his wife Cheryl and their children, Whitney and Andrew. Our church needed something special at the time, and something special is exactly what we got. Ebenezer means rock, and David Hancock has been a rock for our church when we most needed a rock. He has ministered to our church and to our community.

I'm sure that as David reads his name in this column, he trembles with fear about what I might write. You see, David has become on of my favorite targets for practical jokes. He is probably scared to death that I might share one or more of the better ones with the world. But, not to worry, David, I'll not publish what happened when you left your seat at the Braves game, or your response when you got a call from the Rockdale County "Building Authority" concerning preschool improvements. I won't even tell folks how you got out of speaking to the "Young Atlanta Christian Businessmen's Luncheon" so that you could go to Opening Day at Turner Field on April 1.

I won't even harass you about being a Tech fan, because I know you secretly like Georgia and just pull for Georgia Tech to make your daddy mad.

I will say this, however. We hate to see you go. I'm speaking now for the congregation you helped double in size during your short tenure, and the Rockdale community. We understand the nature of the Methodist beast, and will love and support your successor, but we hate to see you go.

I'll also remind you, that on the darkest day of your life, there will be a light shining for you in Conyers--the one you and Cheryl lit in our hearts when you came here. Go in peace, and don't forget the way back. And to Whitney and Andrew, don't forget. You owe me a dollar.

Sweet Salem Spirit
Spans the Generations

*Change, someone once said, is the only constant in life.
One thing I hope never changes is the spirit that prevails
every August when folks return to Salem Campground to
worship, fellowship, and remember.*

Hot! Lord, it was hot! It had been over 100 degrees during the day. The setting of the sun had dropped the temperature a
degree or two, but not much more than that.

I was sitting on a hard wooden bench. My shoes had
been long discarded and my toes were digging into the wooden
shavings beneath them. Sweat was pouring from my brow and
running down my face and into my eyes. My ankles were even
sweating. To tell the truth, I was just about miserable from the
heat --but there's not a place in the world that I would have rather
been last Friday night than at Salem Campground for the start of
the 171st Salem Camp Meeting. Folks have been gathering across
the road from the Salem spring every August since 1828. The
great hand-hewn tabernacle was built a decade before Sherman
passed through. Electricity was added while FDR was president.
For almost 200 summers, good people have worshiped and
fellowshipped here, sang gospel songs, prayed, and listened to
hundreds of preachers.

Camp meetings originated in Kentucky, but were quickly
adopted by the rest of the rural South. They provided a chance for
farmers and their families to gather with others, once the summer
crops were laid by, for fellowship and worship. Most of the annual camp meetings have long since disappeared, giving way to
"progress" and more sophisticated worship services. But to experience a part of the South's heritage, not to mention a taste of the
old time religion, come to the open arbor on Salem Road around
7:45 any night this week.

If you take me up on my offer, be sure to dress comfortably. Don't fret if you have small children. They can play in the shavings on the floor. They've been doing it forever. Several years ago one of the Salem preachers, a big time evangelist from California, took exception to the large number of children in the service. He gave the program director an ultimatum--"Get the children out of the tabernacle, or I'm headed back to Hollywood." It was amazing how quickly he was offered a ride to the airport. He decided to stay. Many of the children who were playing in the sawdust that week still come to Salem. Their children are now playing the shavings, but if that bothers either of this year's preachers, they have not mentioned it.

Salem offers a unique cultural experience. Large crowds of people come from all walks of life, but it's much more than a cultural or social event. Many have found it life changing. Friendships and romances have begun here and countless souls have been saved and redirected. Be forewarned, you'll be hot, but the homemade ice cream served afterward will make up for the heat. Come prepared to be moved spiritually, and plan to come back, year after year, because that's when you really come to understand why Salem is such a special experience.

My mama first brought me to camp meeting while I was still in diapers. I married into a family that tents at Salem and have been fortunate enough to spend the entire week of camp meeting here each of the past 20 years. I see the same families year after year and have watched folks grow up, get married, and bring children of their own here. Of course, every year, there are familiar faces who are no longer with us, and we are reminded that death, too, is a part of life.

One of the faces I've missed this year is that of Mrs. Mary Sue Ramsey. Last year she attended her 100th camp meeting at Salem. That's right! One a year for 100 years. She used to tell me stories about coming to Salem on her daddy's wagon, back before the Wright brothers had first flown an airplane. Mrs. Ramsey, as recently as last August, sat behind me at every service, singing hymns, from memory, with great gusto. She passed away last March.

Last Friday night as we opened camp meeting with our theme song, "Sweet Sweet Spirit," I couldn't help but look over my shoulder, back across the campus toward Mrs. Ramsey's tent, remembering how she used to slowly make her way down the hill. Of course, Mrs. Ramsey wasn't coming down the hill Friday evening, but her grandson was. Joe Cook and his wife, Monica, were pushing a stroller. Riding in the stroller was their 7 month old daughter. Fittingly, her name is Ramsey.

That's why Salem is so special. I have no doubt that in the year 2099, Ramsey Cook and her descendants will be joining my descendants and others on hot August nights to sing the old songs and hear the gospel. As they sit and fan themselves and smile through the heat, they will be encompassed by the same sweet spirit that engulfs those of us who gather now for the last camp meeting of the 20th century.

But I bet they're not as hot as we've been this week.

No Spot Is So Dear

"There's a church in the valley
by the wildwood,
No lovelier spot in the dale;
No place is so dear to my childhood,
As the little brown church in the vale."

That song is by Dr. William Pitts. I used to sing it from the old Cokesbury Hymnal. You remember. The one with the brown cover. I always thought about my church as I sang that song, even though the Julia A. Porter United Methodist Church was not brown, but of red brick and was on a hill instead of in a vale. Of course, when I first started singing that song I didn't know what a vale was.

This weekend I needed to have my picture made for a book I've written that will be released, finally, in a few weeks. It's publication is only two years late, but that's another story. I decided to have the picture made in front of the Methodist Church in

Porterdale.

One might think that having a picture made for a book cover is quite a complex process. I suppose that for some it is, but not for me. I put film in the camera, hand it to my wife, Lisa, and ask her to take my picture. We had a grand old time Sunday afternoon in front of my childhood church. Our photo shoot probably lasted ten or fifteen minutes. We would have finished much sooner but after I had posed for 15 or 20 shots, Lisa realized there was no film in the camera. Once we overcame that obstacle, the wind refused to cooperate. Every time Lisa got ready to snap a picture, the wind would begin to blow what little bit of hair I have left in every direction. We finally got what we hope will be a suitable shot.

We were about to get in our car and leave when I realized that I had not been inside the church in close to twenty years. How could that be? Where does the time go? We decided to go in, but the doors were locked. Hoping I wasn't being a bother, I knocked on the door of the parsonage, which is right beside the church. A gentleman wearing a white dress shirt and tie answered the door. I knew I had the preacher. Nobody else in Porterdale would have on a white shirt and tie at three in the afternoon.

He was very gracious and volunteered to let us in the church before I even asked. He seemed genuinely glad to do it, too. Reverend Davis, which I learned was his name, escorted us around to the side door of the church, the one I was carried through when I was just a few days old to be placed on the Cradle Roll, as the list of Methodist babies was called in Porterdale.

The first thing I spotted was the water fountain. Surely it couldn't have been the same one my daddy held me up to when I was a toddler. I couldn't resist having a drink. The water tasted just the same, cold and pure.

As we walked into the sanctuary I felt at home. Time had gone backward. I looked up at the beautiful vaulted ceiling and remembered all the times when I, as a boy, had tried, unsuccessfully, to count the boards that line the ceiling. I took in the beauty of the arched windows, with the sun shining through the frosted glass. I admired the glorious stained glass window behind the balcony. I sat in one of the pews for a moment.

To my wife and children, and Reverend Davis, the church was empty. But not to me. All around me, on the seemingly empty pews, were the folk I grew up amongst. I could see each one, in their special places.

Marion Johnson was playing the organ. Neil Wheeler was leading the singing. Mrs. Annie Lee Day was in her spot in the choir loft and Red Few was in his. Someone once said that we always had a large and enthusiastic choir at Porterdale. Mrs. Annie was large and Red was enthusiastic.

Mrs. Estelle Allen was right down near the front, on the right side of the church. She may have been the sweetest woman I ever knew. I don't think she ever missed a funeral at our church. I could see Spunk Ivey and his wife Dora in my mind's eye, too. Mr. Ivey was Mayor of Porterdale forever and went over fifty years without missing a Sunday at church. Mrs. Ivey taught me Sunday School and prayed openly that I would make a preacher. I guess she'd be disappointed at how I turned out.

There were so many special people whose presence I felt in that empty church. They were mill people, for the most part, simple and honest and hard working. They came to church and gave their offerings and gave their time, lots of it, to children like me. They helped teach us right from wrong. They taught us important lessons like to turn to the middle of the Bible to find the Psalms, and to close our eyes when we prayed, and that we really needed to pay attention to the red words because they were the ones Jesus spoke. More importantly, they taught us that we were somebody and that we were loved.

I didn't want to take up too much of the preacher's afternoon, so we left before I was really ready to go. As we were leaving, though, I could make out the hymn that the angel choir was singing in my mind. It was Precious Memories. How they linger. How they do linger.

9

Everything's Not Pickrick . . . but it still ain't bad.

Everything's not Pickrick . . .
but it Still Ain't Bad.

Politics, along with religion, are two things that can't bear much discussion without angering people. Therefore, the smart thing, of course, would be to avoid discussing religion and politics. Usually, I do. Usually, but not always.

I've always had a keen interest in politics, even before I understood much about them. My father used to tell stories about Eugene Talmadge and his son, Herman, and Richard B. Russell, that Georgia giant of the U.S. Senate. Later I had the privilege of meeting many of our state leaders in person. I've never been invited to dinner at the White House, but I once road down Peachtree Street with Lester Maddox in a Model A Ford on the Fourth of July. It's hard to top an experience like that.

I've found myself on the unpopular side of many political fences, but never let it be said that I have ever been a mugwump, which is a gutless creature that sits on a fence with its mug on one side and its wump on the other. I have always been one to take a stand for things I believe to be right.

My daddy was a yellow dog Democrat. He would vote for a yellow dog if it were running on a Democratic ticket. I'm not and I wouldn't. I'm not sure I'm a Republican, either, although I'm a lot closer to Ronald Reagan than Bill Clinton.

Whatever I am, I am not afraid to express my opinion, so hold onto your hat and proceed with caution.

We Baby Boomers Have Arrived

If you are a fan of Bill Clinton's, you should probably just move on to the next selection. Of course, if you're a fan of Bill Clinton's, you probably stopped reading this book a long time ago, if you ever started at all.

I was in Athens recently at a social studies conference. A bad day in Athens is better than a good day most other places. The keynote speaker at my conference had a world of charts and statistics about the demographics of American's population. I was startled to realize that my generation-- the Baby Boomers--is now firmly ensconced in middle age. I'm older that my father used to be. I'll never play center field for the Yankees. My generation in middle age! How did we ever get there?

The startling realization that my bald spot is growing proportionately to my belt size started me to thinking about comparisons between my generation and that of our parents. Our mamas and daddies were heroes. They lived through a depression and fought Hitler. Beat him, too.

They ate buttermilk and cornbread and cooked at home. They saved their money and paid cash. They placed a value on truth and honor. They promised a brighter future for their children--and delivered.

I began to consider the common experiences that make my generation unique. We were the first to grow up with television. Captain Kangaroo and Howdy Doody were our childhood friends.

We stood in line at the school cafeteria to eat a sugar cube so we wouldn't get polio. Doctors came to our house and gave us penicillin shots when we took sick. We watched Mickey Mantle and Willie Mays and Johnny Unitas. We cherished their performances on the field and didn't care what they did when the game was over.

My generation was scared to death by the threat of nuclear

war. We saw Nikita Khrushchev pound a table and promise to bury us. We knew people who had fallout shelters. We lived through the Cuban Missile Crisis. In the fifth grade, during the height of the Cuban scare, we had a nuclear attack drill during school every day for weeks. Miss Mary Tripp made us sit under our desks and cover our heads. Miss Mary Tripp was one of the best teachers at Porterdale School but she obviously didn't know beans about nuclear bombs.

We, the Baby Boomers, watched transfixed as John Glenn orbited the earth. We saw the world stop for three days when a president was killed. We were the generation which realized that there were inequalities in our society that couldn't be tolerated and did something about it. We realized that the earth had a finite amount of natural resources and began to try and conserve them. We protested a war that we didn't believe in. We turned up our noses at cornbread and buttermilk and started drinking bottled water.

For years we were told by our teachers that we would be the leaders of tomorrow. Wouldn't you know it? Our teachers were right. Tomorrow is here and we are the leaders.

We are movers and shakers. We are surgeons and firemen and Baptist deacons. We are teachers and school board members and CEOs. And for the first time, the leader of the free world is one of us. And he's now standing trial for perjury and obstruction of justice. He has been impeached. Everyone agrees he did what he's accused of and are now merely haggling over a fitting punishment.

Doesn't that make a person stop to think? Is our president, with his apparent lack of moral judgement and penchant for disregarding the truth, reflective of our whole generation?

I have a friend from Harlan, Ky. Harlan is in the coal mining region of Appalachia. People there, by necessity, are cut from a different bolt of cloth. One day I was returning from St. Simons Island and stopped to buy gas at a station on the expressway. As I was filling my tank I noticed a Kentucky tag on the car beside mine. Just to be neighborly I tried to strike up a conversation with the owner of the Kentucky car. "I see you're from Kentucky," I said. "I have a good friend from Harlan, Kentucky."

The stranger looked at me with ice cold eyes and said, "Don't judge the whole state of Kentucky by a man from Harlan." He screwed on his gas cap and went inside to pay.

That applies here. Don't judge an entire generation by one president from Arkansas. The Baby Boomers aren't all like him. Are we?

Everything Was Pickrick Under the Gold Dome

Lester Maddox is, without a doubt, one of the most contro-versial politicians in our state's history. He is also one of the most honest. With Lester Maddox, what you see is what you get. He was, truly, one of a kind. I'm proud to say he was my friend.

There we were under the great gold dome. The whole Huckaby clan was gathered beneath the rotunda, inside the Georgia State Capitol in Atlanta. We were there by special invitation from the State Department of Transportation. I have to admit, I was a bit nervous when I got a letter in the mail from the DOT. I was afraid they had found out I was with the guys that stole that stop sign from Dixie Road in 1968.

They hadn't. We were invited to a special ceremony dedicating the Lester and Virginia Maddox Bridge, which spans the Chattahoochee River on I-75. What a great location. That bridge separates Cobb and Fulton Counties. Half the people in America cross that bridge on their way to Disney World. The other half cross it to come into Atlanta to work every day. The sign on the bridge will be seen, understand. No one deserves the honor more than our former governor and his lovely first lady. I mean that.

I know that Lester Maddox was a segregationist past the

time it was fashionable. George Washington owned slaves but I haven't noticed anybody refusing to spend dollar bills with his picture on them. Let me go ahead and say what many of the self righteous among us are thinking. How could they honor such a man by naming a bridge after him? I know he closed his Pickrick Restaurant rather than integrate it, depriving all of us, by the way, of some of the best fried chicken in the world. I know about the axe handles, too, except they were pick handles. Unfortunately, that is all most people know about Lester Maddox. They know the Lester Maddox portrayed by the media, and that's all. Most don't know the man, or his true record.

I first met Lester Maddox in 1968. He walked into my American History class, unannounced, and told all of us what a great country we lived in. He also told us to behave ourselves and mind our teacher and try to learn. Now I teach American History. Lord, I wish the governor would walk into my classroom and tell my students to behave themselves and mind me. Over the years I was fortunate enough to become good friends with this man and have learned an awful lot about him. Much of it is public record, much is not.

When Lester Maddox was chosen to be governor by the General Assembly of Georgia, many people openly feared that he would embarrass himself and his state. Nothing could have been further from the truth. The only people he embarrassed were the folks who had to take their hand out of the public till and the people who could no longer dictate state policy. Lester Maddox ran the most open and honest administration in the history of this state. You can look it up.

One day a week he opened his office to anyone who wanted to come in and talk. Have you tried walking into the governor's office and having a chat lately? He reformed our prisons and did away with the chain gang. He gave teachers, among the most poorly paid in the nation at that time, a 25% pay raise over his four year tenure and the so called racist appointed more black Georgians to state positions, including white collar jobs, than all governors before him combined. I'm not politicking. I don't think Lester Maddox is running again. I'm just stating facts.

The special day last week was not for dredging up the past. It was meant to honor the accomplishments of a truly good man and to honor the memory of his partner of "61 years, one month, fourteen days, fifteen hours, and 40 minutes"—this according to the governor himself. There were dignitaries galore. Guy Sharpe was there and so was the Reverend Norman Price. Commissioner of Agriculture and former Maddox campaign manager, Tommy Irving, spoke. So did Lt. Governor Mark Taylor. There's a lot of him to speak. Others made speeches, too. Roy Barnes sent a letter. All the people who spoke used words like character and honesty and decency. Those words don't ring true with enough of today's politicians.

The day clearly belonged to Lester Maddox and he was bouncing around the capitol in his seersucker suit as if it were 1966 and he was about to roam the state nailing Maddox Country signs to south Georgia pine trees. His energy and enthusiasm belied his 82 years and his six bouts with cancer. It was vintage Maddox, a reminder of a bygone day in Georgia politics.

Bubba McDonald closed the festivities by singing *God Bless America*, at Governor Maddox's request. That ol' boy can sing. We all joined in on the chorus, and for a few minutes, at least, believed that America would, indeed, be blessed.

By the way. Hosea Williams was in attendance, along with his driver, I hope. Somewhere along the line he and Lester Maddox took time to know one another and found out they had much more in common than they had differences. They are very close friends. Imagine that. I guess a bridge is a pretty good symbol with which to honor Lester Maddox, after all. He built a lot of them. More than most people will ever take time to know.

Controversy or Not—Here I Come

*Nothing has changed concerning this topic since this
column was first published, including my opinion.*

This is a mistake. I know it's a mistake. I know I should
not delve into this topic. Subjects such as who serves the best
barbecue and which state university has bribed the best teenaged
athletes to play football cause enough controversy. I know I will
offend some people. Others will not be able to see my position to
save their collective lives. Some will call me names and demand
my head on a platter.

Having said all that, let me say this. I don't care. This is
an opinion column and I have a right to express mine, even if it is
not politically correct and even if it some don't agree with me. It
won't be the first time that's happened.

Thursday afternoon President Michael Adams of the
University of Georgia announced that, despite court rulings against
the practice, the University of Georgia would continue to use race
as a criteria for acceptance to my beloved Alma Mater. I think he
was wrong.

Let the onslaught begin. But before you call me a racist
and a demagogue and accuse me of being a member of the Ku
Klux Klan, at least hear me out.

First of all, let me say that I am not against any qualified
person attending the University of Georgia. Even as I type these
words—by the way—do we still type, even if we don't use a type-
writer? Probably not. Sorry. Got sidetracked. Even as I process
these words I know some will say, "That racist so and so doesn't
want African American students at the University of Georgia. That
just isn't so, and just because I disagree with President Adams's
decision doesn't mean that I am against people of any ethnic background being admitted to our state's flagship university. I just
don't want them to get preferential treatment.

I was born during the time of a segregated South. As I
grew up, so did the region. I lived through the integration of

schools, restaurants, and society in general. I have been able to see, as I've grown older and hopefully wiser, that many people I still respect and admire were on the wrong side of that issue. I've spent time on the wrong side of it myself. I don't believe for one minute that I'm wrong now.

I lived through a day when many people, including some of our highest elected officials, insisted that black students were intellectually inferior to white students. The first time I had a black classmate was in the ninth grade. Due to the luck of an alphabetical seating chart a girl named Sandra Hollingsworth, a recent transfer from the all black R.L. Cousins High School, sat right in front of me. It took about one test for Sandra to blow the theory of intellectual inferiority right out of the water. She was way smarter than me. She's a doctor now, by the way, if you need more evidence than one Algebra test.

I know what the black students went through who integrated our schools. They were looked upon as trouble makers. They were mocked and ridiculed and worse. Looking back on those days, they were some of the bravest people I have ever known. They were pioneers. They were hand chosen, during the days of separate but equal, to prove that they and theirs deserved to be treated as equals. Even during those misguided days of my youth I believed that. I still do. That is why I am against Dr. Adams's decision.

I believe that he is demeaning the African American students in Georgia's schools. I believe that he is saying to them, "We realize that you can't produce on the same level as students of other ethnic backgrounds, so we don't expect as much out of you."

What kind of message does that send? Where is the justice in telling one student who has an A average and an SAT score of a thousand points, "Sorry, you don't qualify. Of course the person in the seat beside you who has a lower score and lower GPA does qualify because, well, their skin tone is different, and their people haven't had the cultural advantages your people have had."

Dress it up any way you want to, that's what Dr. Adams is saying.

We've spent too long telling children and young people that they aren't capable. We've lowered standards; we've lowered expectations; we've made allowances—for people of all colors. When you expect less and accept less, you'd better believe you get less.

It's time we judge people on their ability. It's time we expect the best of all people. It's time we raise our expectations and reward those who achieve regardless of race or gender. It's time we judge people "not by the color of their skin, but by the content of their character." Didn't Dr. King say that? Didn't he die for promoting that opinion. Doesn't it apply to everyone?

Sorry if I offended anyone, but that's my opinion, and I'm sticking to it.

An Eye Opening Experience Under the Gold Dome

I'm glad I didn't spend too much time at the state capitol on this visit. After seeing the legislation passed by this year's General Assembly, I have decided that I was in a scarier place that I had realized.

I took a trip to the Gold Dome the other morning. I was interested in talking first hand to some of our esteemed state legislators about the governor's education reform bill. I'm all for any measure that will improve education in Georgia, or anywhere else for that matter. I just wanted to hear for myself that our current crop of lawmakers didn't intend to throw the baby out with the bath water in what seems like the inevitable passage of the governor's much discussed overhauling of our public schools.

I was reminded as I observed our General Assembly in action of the old adage that if a fellow ever watches laws or sausage being made, he'll never care for either again. I can say a hearty "amen" to that.   I couldn't believe the way those folks were wandering around, reading the newspaper, and carrying on conversations, seemingly oblivious to people who were making speeches on important issues. If my civics class acted like those legislators, I'd have them all in detention. It wasn't long before I had seen enough and decided to take a walk and admire the newly refurbished building.

Although I have made many trips to the capitol I am always impressed by the history that permeates the building, although I've heard it said that at one time, more legislation was passed in the smoke filled rooms of the old Henry Grady Hotel than on the floor of the legislature. I enjoyed my little tour of the building, although I missed being able to see the two headed calf that once graced the museum on the top level.

I couldn't help but pause and admire the bust of James Edward Oglethorpe, who founded Georgia nearly three centuries ago. His original idea was to form a colony for debtors between the Savannah and Altamaha rivers. If everybody that lives between those rivers today spends money like my wife, I'd say that General Oglethorpe pretty much got his wish. Somebody stole her charge card last summer. I didn't report it for three months because the person that stole it spent way less than she did.

I also spent some time in front of the portrait of former governor Lester Maddox. There he was in his seersucker suit with a portrait of his beloved wife Virginia in a frame on the desk he was standing beside. I couldn't help but grin, again, at the large mullet in the picture, wrapped securely in the Atlanta Constitution, which the governor often proclaimed was only fit for wrapping fish. He should see it now.

There were several Confederate battle flags in display cases in the capitol. Real ones that had been carried into battle by real men, many of whom left home never to return, and many of whom returned to the burned out remnants of what had once been home. I couldn't help but wonder how they would feel about the furor being caused by their once proud flag.

It was such a beautiful day that I decided to walk outside

and admire the grounds of our statehouse. No one had told the flowers or the trees that it was almost spring, but it was nice to be outside, anyway. I took time to examine many of the statues that surround the building. I paid homage to Governor Joseph Brown and his wife, General John B. Gordon, and, of course, Tom Watson. Jimmy Carter was in a place of honor, wearing a work shirt with the sleeves rolled up, which is somehow appropriate for the peanut farmer who would be president.

I finally got around to the southeast corner of the grounds. There stood my very favorite sculpture—former governor Eugene Talmadge, feet braced, finger pointing, shock of hair falling down over his forehead, and, naturally, coat thrown back to reveal his trademark red suspenders.

I stared into the bronze face of that great populist politician and then read the inscription on the base of the monument. It was a quote from Gene's own lips. "I may surprise you, but I'll never deceive you."

They don't make politicians like Gene Talmadge anymore. He was a champion of the little man, especially the little man who lived in rural Georgia. During the days of the county--unit system, in which a vote in Taliaferro County was worth ten or twenty in Fulton, he made no secret of the fact that he didn't care if he ever got a vote in a district that had street car tracks.

He was elected governor four times, the first on the promise of a three dollar automobile tag, which would have been a boon to poor Georgia cotton farmers during the height of the depression. When the state legislature refused to go along with the new governor's proposal, he found an obscure state statute that gave the governor the right to suspend any part of any tax during a state of emergency. It didn't take Ol' Gene long to create an emergency and suspend all tax on car tags—except three dollars.

The poor dirt farmers who gave him his political base believed him when he said, "You only have three friends in this world you can trust—God, Sears-Roebuck, and Gene Talmadge."

My daddy used to enjoy telling the story of the time he informed an old clod buster at a country store over in Arnoldsville that the state was going to move Stone Mountain.

"Ain't no way in tarnation they could move that big old rock," said the farmer.

"Gene Talmadge said they were," responded my daddy.

"Reckon where they're gonna put it?" was the old man's reply.

No. They don't make politicians like that anymore. I started to go back inside the capitol after my visit with Eugene Talmadge's statue, but decided against it. I had seen enough for one day.

By the way, I don't plan on taking any field trips to the sausage factory anytime soon. I decided after watching our legislature in session that there are some things we're better off not knowing.

10

Were the Good Old Days as Good as We Remember?

Were the Good Old Days as Good as We Remember?

Those were the days, weren't they? How many times have we all said that? For me, the good old days took place in a four room house in the mill village of Porterdale. We had lino-leum floors and no closets. A space heater in the living room provided heat for that room and the kitchen. Layers of hand sewn quilts provided heat for the bedroom, as long as you stayed under them.

The bathroom was outside. A bare bulb hanging down from the ceiling in each room provided light. Their was no such thing as air conditioning, at least not as far as we knew. The tele-vision was black and white and could pick up three channels. The radio was AM and the telephone was a party line.

The car was second hand. The city limits of Porterdale was our entire world most of the time. A trip to town was a big deal. Movies were a dime and Cokes were a nickel. They came in little green bottles.

Eating out was unheard of. Home cooked meals were a given--every night. We could, and did, play all over the village and only had to report in at meal times and at dark. Nobody wor-ried about where we were or what we were doing, nor did they need to. Our schools were friendly and safe. Our teachers always had the last say and paddled our bottoms when they needed pad-dling.

Were the good old days really that good? Yeah. I believe they were. Come now, with me, and lets play "remember when . . .?"

Clothes Make the Person? . . .
Lord I Hope Not!

Fashion, if anything, has taken a turn for the worse since this was published.

I'm fixin to do something my mama told me never to do. (If I were from a more sophisticated region of our great nation I would say, "I'm about to go against the lifetime advice of my mother." But, since I'm a proud son of the South, I'm fixin' to do something my mama told me never to do.) I'm gonna talk about people's clothes.

My mama was a child of the Depression. She was one of four children being raised by a single mom before it became fashionable. Her dresses were homemade hand-me-downs which she felt fortunate to have. She constantly reminded me that whatever a person wore was probably the best they had, and if she ever caught me making fun of someone's clothes she'd send me out to cut a switch.

Despite that long-standing warning, I'm still fixin' to make fun of folks' clothes because today's teen fashions are, well, funny. At least to me. Have you been to a mall or other teen hangout lately? The platform shoes girls wear should come with a parachute so if they fall off their shoes they'll at least have a chance at survival. My 13-year-old daughter has footwear so ugly they'd make bowling shoes look stylish.

Teenage girls are also heavy into skintight polyester pants with flared bottoms. They come in purple and orange and neon green and are worn with tops two sizes too small and bare midriffs. The midriffs are bare to accentuate the belly button rings. If anyone can explain to me why someone would poke a hole through a perfectly intact navel, I'm willing to listen.

As bad as teen girl fashions are, boys' styles may be worse. I've gotten used to baseball caps being turned around backward. If everyone wants to go around looking like Yogi Berra, so be it.

But I'll never get used to guys wearing blue jeans with legs big enough for a family of four. And these elephant-sized pants are worn so low they defy gravity. The inseam winds up at the knees. I understand that's called "bustin' slack." For those teenagers who think they invented the style, I was bustin' slack 40 years ago, but not on purpose.

I was in the third-grade and had outgrown the one pair of overalls I wore to school every day. Mama told me to stop by the store and get a new pair on the way to school. The dry goods store in Porterdale opened at 7 a.m. so people on the third shift at the mill could shop on their way home. In our wonderful little town a 9-year-old could shop on his own and sign the ticket. But there was a problem this particular morning. The only overalls available were three sizes too large. The sales clerk, who I'm sure worked on commission, insisted they were perfect.

Promising me that I'd grow into them, he rolled up the cuffs and sent me off to school. Everyone else at Porterdale School had mamas who wore hand-me-downs during the Depression, too. Nobody mentioned my pants and all was well until recess. We had a giant sliding board on our playground and the real fun of the sliding board was to wait until the teacher wasn't looking and then to slide down one of the long poles that held it up--fireman style. I climbed the steps of the slide and waited until my teacher was watching the girls on the jungle gym. I climbed out on the support pole and slid. The excessive material of my pants got caught on a bolt. I wound up on the ground in my step-ins and my overalls were still at the top of the slide. Naturally every child on the playground had chosen that precise moment to turn their collective attention to the sliding board. I started running and didn't stop until I was safely inside my mama's kitchen.

I begged my parents to move to a new town, but they wouldn't.

A word of advice to today's teenage boys. Wear what you want, but don't go near the sliding board.

By the way, after reading the first draft of this article, my daughter, Jamie, rummaged through some boxes in the attic and came up with a picture of me taken in 1971. I believe I was on my way to a Three Dog Night concert. I was nattily attired in bright orange-and-white-striped polyester pants, bell bottoms, of course. The skintight shirt perfectly matched my 3 inch platform shoes and my sideburns would have made Elvis envious.

Hmmmmmm. I think I'll go hang out at the mall. These new fashions are pretty cool.

Longing for Just One Snow Day

Two winters have passed since this column was published. We've had half a dozen close calls and two ice storms . . . but no snow.

It's just not fair. Like every January, thousands across the metro area have listened to and watched every weather forecast, hoping against hope for that rare Georgia snowfall that would close schools and give everyone an unplanned holiday from math and science classes, homework, pop quizzes and school food.

And those are just the teachers. The kids would probably enjoy a snow day, too.

Every week the weather guys (and girls) tease us with the "S" word in their trailers. Then they make us stay tuned for further details. We sit and watch the news all through the dinner hour to learn that Tennessee and North Carolina and Minnesota will get snow.

The north Georgia mountains will get a dusting. Metro Atlanta? A possible trace with no accumulation. Where's the justice in that?

Don't get me wrong. I'm not demanding or even hoping for a blizzard. I know when I've got it good. I thank the Lord every night I wasn't born in Buffalo or Cleveland or anywhere else in the frozen tundra north of Nashville. But every couple of years a nice blanket of white would be nice. Just enough to create a siege mentality, sending everybody to Kroger for bread and milk and closing everything down for a day or two. Who can forget the joy of an unexpected snowstorm?

Back before we had 3-D weather and satellites and all the modern equipment that enables our meteorologists to track the first trace of frozen precipitation from its conception, snow would sneak up on us every now and again. Wasn't it wonderful? You go to sleep--nothing. Wake up. It looks like a Christmas card outside. Everyone sits by the radio straining to hear their school system listed among the closings.

As soon as you heard that school had been cancelled you put on every piece of warm clothing you owned and headed out to make snow angels, build snowmen, seek out opponents for snowball fights and find a hill to slide down.

Of course we knew what to do in the snow. We'd all seen it on TV and in books. But we in the South had to make some concessions to the fact that snow was such a rarity. For instance, there were no mittens or gloves in my whole town. We wore socks on our hands to protect them from the cold. It took about two snowballs for them to be soaking wet and colder than bare hands.

Naturally there were no sleds in Porterdale, but cardboard was a passable substitute. We never seemed to have the right kind of snow for making snowmen, which was just as well because we wouldn't have had top hats or scarves to decorate them with any way. But we would stay outside all day, never thinking about complaining of being cold or wet. Surprise snowstorms were one of the jewels that made childhood such a precious treasure and, unfortunately, seem to have gone the way of Guy Sharp and record players.

OK. No more surprise winter storms for the metro area. We'll take a planned one. Let all the television and radio stations tell us about it days in advance. Let them all claim to have been the first with the forecast and the most accurate. Just let it snow.

It used to snow. Remember Snowjam? I want to see big flakes falling out of the sky. I want to watch the ground get covered. I want to build a giant fire and cook a pot of chili all day. I want the pleasure of waking my kids with the news, "It's snow-ing!" and then watch the excitement on their faces as they scurry around to put on all the warm clothes they can find. I won't even complain when they come in and out of the house a dozen times, strewing water and wet clothes.

I'll tell you how badly I want snow. I won't even mind hearing all the Yankee-Americans who have infiltrated our part of the world laugh at how excited we get over winter weather, and I'll only get a little mad when they continue to harp at us about not being able to drive on icy roads.

Which reminds me. I was watching the weather last night and schools were closed in Buffalo--because of snow. I also saw footage of lots of snow-related car wrecks in Illinois and Michigan. I guess Southern drivers went up there and caused them.

Meanwhile--think snow and happy sledding!

An Evening at the Movies . . . '90s Style

The features keep getting worse and prices keep getting higher. On our last foray to the movies we took the kids and spent $57.50 for tickets, Cokes, and popcorn for five. That's more than twice what the British paid for New York. Come to think of it, maybe we got a better deal, after all.

My wife decided that we would go to the movies the other day. That's not something we do often. The last time we went to the movies, in fact, the film was in black and white and didn't involve talking. Well, maybe it hasn't been that long, but you get the point.

When I was growing up in Porterdale, you had to go to town if you wanted to go to "the Show," as we called it. Going to town meant going to Covington to the Strand Theater. Now that was a movie house!

I think it cost a quarter. If you said "please" and "thank you," when you bought your ticket, Mrs. Brownie Osborne, the owner of the theater and ticket seller, would often give you a free pass. Mrs. Brownie Osborne appreciated politeness.

Usually I had money for popcorn and a Coke. You didn't get free popcorn for saying "please" and "thank you," but we all did it anyway, because we were brought up right. I can't remember the exact cost of the refreshments, but I'm pretty sure 15 cents covered both items.

The Strand Theater had a special section of seats in back where couples could sit. It was dark as a dungeon in that area, and I'm not sure what went on because I never had the nerve to sit there. I was scared enough that Foy Harper would shine his flashlight on me and tell me to "shush" while sitting in the relative safety of the regular seats. That was Foy's job. He was the usher. He would tear your tickets as you came in and then patrol the aisles during the movie. Heaven forbid anyone talk during the feature presentation. If one did, that person had to deal with Foy, who weighed all of 100 pounds, but ruled the aisles of the Strand Theater with an iron fist--or--flashlight, as the case may be.

I saw some great movies at the Strand Theater in Covington, and they were all preceded by a cartoon and one or two previews. There was only one movie per week. The movies weren't rated, but they didn't need to be. The most violence I ever saw was John Wayne shooting Indians and bad guys. The most titillating thing was Annette Funicello in a two-piece swim suit.

I don't remember all the movies I saw at the Strand, but many do stand out. I remember seeing "The Blob" and being scared to death for months that a great glob of gunk would roll right over Porterdale and take away every person and house. I saw Elvis movies at the Strand and Walt Disney classics like "Peter Pan" and "Bambi" and "Toby Tyler Joins the Circus".

I even saw *Gone With the Wind* at the Strand Theater. I was the ninth grade and had finally gotten up enough nerve to ask a girl to meet me at the movie. The young lady, who shall remain nameless, was from Covington, and was developed far beyond her years. I'm not talking intellect, either. I showed up on Friday night to view Margaret Mitchell's classic tale of the Old South convinced that I would receive an education, in more ways than one.

Sure enough, no sooner had Scarlett said "yes" to her first husband than the young lady I was sitting with was holding my hand. By the time Rhett danced with Scarlett at the bazaar, she was snuggled against my shoulder. Wouldn't you know it! An emergency had arisen at home. My sister had decided to go to South Carolina and get married to my brother-in-law, who was being sent to Vietnam in 36 hours. My mother had come, in person, to the Strand Theater to fetch me home. Just as I was about to put my arm around my companion's shoulder, which would have been a first for me, the powerful beam of Foy Harper's flashlight landed right on me. Sometimes at night I can still hear Foy's voice saying, "Here he is, Mrs. Huckaby. I found him. He's down here with a girl."

Drat my luck. By the time I got up enough nerve to ask another girl to meet me at the show, the Strand Theater was a mere memory.

I did indeed take my wife to the movies. We drove 30 miles to a giant theater with stadium seating and surround sound. It cost more than a quarter to get in. I said "please" and "thank you." The ticket seller called me a wise guy and didn't mention a free pass. I could feed my family for a week on what they wanted for Coke and popcorn. Thank goodness the concession stand took credit cards.

There were 16 movies to choose from. The Strand didn't show 16 movies in four months. They were rated everything from *G* to *can't-say-in-a-family-newspaper.* We saw *Notting Hill.* There was no cartoon, but they did show 37 previews. The movie was semi-funny. Julia Roberts was the star. She was pretty to look at, but she didn't have a thing on Annette, and Annette never talked ugly.

All in all, we had a good time and may even go back some-time, if we win the lottery.

Today's Society Needs More Mama-isms

I still quote my mama--and my kids still just roll their eyes.

Like all good Southern boys, I was raised up doing what my mama said. My mama, like most I suppose, had a few things she told me over and over and over. Her mama probably told them to her. I call them mama-isms. I'm not sure they are in such wide spread use today. I never hear my wife use any of them with our kids.

I wonder when American mothers turned away from mama-isms. I bet it was about the same time they started putting the Andy Griffith Show on in color and tried to replace the irreplaceable Barney Fife with Warren. Remember Warren? He came in about the same time the designated hitter did, and did about as much for the Mayberry police force as the DH did for the American League.

I believe we'd be better off if we brought back some mama-isms, and made our kids pay attention to them. Like, "Being nice don't cost a thing and is worth a fortune," or "Please and thank you will take you further than a Cadillac, for a lot less money."

I was told every day, "You say 'Yes, Ma'am' and 'No Ma'am.' I don't want folks thinking you're a Yankee child."

Did you ever hear, "Don't run with a sharp stick. You'll put your eye out?" That was one of my favorites. I have scoured newspapers nearly every day of my life looking for one mention of an incident in which a kid actually put his eye out by running with a sharp stick. I've yet to find one, but it still sounds like something good to tell kids not to do.

One that my mother said to me every time I ever left home in my whole life was, "You better behave yourself. You never know who might be watching you." You know, my mama was absolutely right about that. No matter how far I travel, I always run into someone I know. Whenever I do, my first thought is, "I hope I was behaving myself when they saw me. I'd hate for word to get back to my mama that I wasn't."

Another mama-ism from my youth was, "walking ain't crowded." This was one she used when I would ask her to take me somewhere that was within easy walking distance—say, six or seven miles.

If I ever indicated that I was afraid to stay by myself at night her advice would be to "strike a match" if anyone bothered me. I think the implication was that my ugliness would scare anyone away who intended to do me bodily harm. This included the boogy man and the Soap Sally. It was before the days of home intrusions, but come to think of it, I've never been accosted in a dark room. This mama-ism was a direct contradiction of another favorite, "Act as good as you look and you'll do fine."

"You're old enough for your wants not to hurt you," indicated that no matter what movie star or athlete endorsed an item that I didn't need, I wasn't getting it.

Of course, one mama-ism used by mothers everywhere was "always wear clean underwear in case you're in a wreck." I was, in fact, in a wreck once. The condition of my underwear didn't cross my mind and none of the doctors or nurses mentioned it, in a positive or negative way. Speaking of clean underwear reminds me of a mama-ism my grandmother used to use. I guess that would make it a grandma-ism. She always assured us that whatever we were scared of, be it snake, spider, or barking dog was always more afraid of us than we were of it.

I was staying with my grandmama one summer. We were having a drought and the well was dry so she sent me to the creek to get a bucket of drinking water. When I got to the creek, a big ol' snake was sunning itself, right where I needed to fill up my bucket. Needless to say, I returned to the house with an empty bucket.

My grandmother, naturally, wanted to know why I didn't get the water.

I said, "Granny, I couldn't get any water. There was a big ol' snake down at the creek and I was scared of it.

She replied, using her favorite mama-ism, "That snake is

as scared of you as you are of it."

I assured her that if that were the case, that water wouldn't be fit to drink anyway.

If my mama finds out I told that story she will probably use another favorite. "I'm gonna wear you out when I get you home."

Lord, she would, too.

I'm not sure what mama-isms today's soccer moms use to make sure their children grow up to be decent, respectful folks. I hope one that never goes out of style is the one that none of us can hear too often. "I love you, son. You know I love you."

Thankfully, I always did know that—and still do.

Take Your Shoes Off . . . If You Dare

I got thank-you notes from several drug stores after this column appeared. It seems that Band-aid and methylate sales skyrocketed in the area.

Whatever happened to going barefoot? I went out to Porterdale to visit my mother last weekend and she reminded me that it was May 1, which was always the magic day for being allowed to go without shoes. It didn't matter if it were 97 degrees on April 30, those shoes better be on your feet when you walked out the door. By contrast, On May 1, be it a hundred degrees or be it 48 degrees, as it was last Saturday, bare feet were fine.

Looking back on my childhood, it's hard to remember why going without my shoes was something I wanted to do so badly. It might have been that we only got one pair of shoes per school year. Mine were always of the brown brogan variety. We bought them at the beginning of school and they lasted until summer, no matter how many sizes my feet grew. It might have been just getting relief for my toes that made being without footwear so appealing. Porterdale was the sandspur capitol of the world in those days. It was impossible to wander the village without getting one's feet stuck a hundred times. Usually the more agile among us could stand on one foot and pick the sandspurs out of the other. If you happened to get them in both feet at the same time you just balanced on the edge of one foot. You knew you had a bad case of the stickers if you ever had to sit down to pick your feet. Sitting, of course, created the possibility of getting sandspurs in your bottom. You'd find out who your real friends were when you got a backside full of sandspurs and needed help removing them.

During the summer months, the washing of feet, removal of imbedded stickers, and swabbing of said feet with hydrogen peroxide was an evening ritual performed all over our little mill village. A kid might go several days between tub baths, but no child in Porterdale ever went to bed with dirty feet.

Sandspurs weren't the only affliction awaiting the barefoot children of Porterdale. We also had to worry about the dreaded stubbed toe. I'm not sure today's children even know what a stubbed toe is. I'm not talking about a little garden variety, "Oh, I stubbed my toe." That doesn't even qualify. I'm talking about a running full speed, didn't pick my foot up high enough over the curb, black and blue, nearly broken, blood everywhere, red medicine and six Band-Aids, stubbed toe. If you've never had one, you wouldn't understand. It's impossible to put into words how painful they were. About one a week was my summertime average.

In addition to sandspurs and stubbed toes barefoot children had to deal with hot pavement, stepping on an occasional piece of glass, or a serious burn from some inconsiderate person who threw a cigarette down without crushing it under the heel of his or her shoe. The fact that Porterdale had a large population of stray dogs added a whole different risk to summertime.

We live on a farm and there are no sandspurs that I'm aware of. Neither are there curbs, broken glass, cigarette butts, or hot pavement, but my kids still don't go outside barefoot. One reason is that they have so many pairs of shoes, it would be a shame not to wear them as much as possible. Today's kids have shoes for school, shoes for church, shoes for playing in mud, and shoes for playing on sunny days; not to mention soccer shoes, basketball shoes, ballet shoes, clogs, flip-flops, and water shoes.

Of course, there is a shoe monster that lives in our house and invariably picks on the youngest child, who may not go outside barefoot, but never wears shoes in the house. And it never fails that when we are ready to go somewhere the little one can only find one shoe. Tolstoy could have written War and Peace in the time I've spent looking for one shoe. There are two rules concerning shoe searches. Rule number one. The time it takes to find the shoe is directly and inversely related to the amount of time you have to get where you are going. The later you are and the more important the engagement the longer it will take to find the shoe. I had to petition my church to start Sunday School twenty minutes later because I could never find my child's shoe.

The other rule is that the shoe will invariably turn up in the most illogical place it could possibly be and the child will never have had anything to do with its disappearance.

If my reminiscing about the good old days has made you nostalgic, go ahead and take your shoes off and go outside. My mama says it's all right. But be careful where you step and don't stub your toe. Band-Aids and peroxide are more expensive than they used to be.

It's Summer—At Last

We survived the summer of '99, but barely. After travelling to Maine, Niagara Falls, Myrtle Beach, and the north Georgia mountains, we were all ready for school to start back. We needed the rest.

Just two more days and sounds of jubilation will ring out across Rockdale County. From Milstead to Magnet and all points in between, teachers will shout for joy. Students might celebrate, too.

I once was accused of going into teaching just so I would have the summers off. Not true. There were many reasons I became an educator. June, July, and August were just three of them. Of course, these days you can scratch August from your list of benefits. I must admit, I do enjoy summer. But not as much as I used to when I was growing up in Porterdale.

Summers then, of course, began around Memorial Day and ended after Labor Day. They seemed eternal. My kids have so many activities that my family can hardly squeeze in a week at the beach or a camping trip. Heaven forbid we miss something. Especially not a camp.

My kids go to church camp, Cub Scout camp, cheerleading camp, basketball camp, dance camp, academic camp, music camp—you name it, there is a camp for it. Of course, few, if any, involve a tent or staying overnight. I don't know when our society became so dependent on camps for our kids, but I think it was somewhere between Mickey Mantle and Dennis Rodman.

Every activity my kids are involved in this summer requires three things. One is a registration form. It was easier to register for the draft than Cheerleader Camp. For Vacation Bible School, which isn't called camp, yet, but I'm sure one day will be, we had to register three months in advance. Dance camp registration required a signature in blood.

The second thing about each activity is they all cost money. A great deal of money, actually. I'm glad my parents didn't have to pay for me to become enriched and entertained all summer. If they had, I would have been out of luck. The combined fees we are paying for all our kids' camps is more than the gross national product of several small countries. Combined!

The third thing about these activities is that adults are 100% in charge of organizing and administering them. Sometimes it's hard to tell if the activity is meant to benefit the child or the adults.

Of course, all of the activities require that children be dropped off and picked up in automobiles. I think it's a law that if a family has more than one child, at least two children must be involved in activities which begin and end at the exact same time, in diametrically opposite ends of the county.

Oh, for the good old days when I was a poor little disadvantaged mill child. We had activities, too. Whatever we got together and decided to do was our activity.

We played baseball during the mornings. No uniforms. No coaches. No helmets or dugouts or pitching machines or fences with advertising. We just played. For hours. Sometimes it was only five to a side. Hit it to right field, you're out. If there weren't enough for a game we played roller bat or push up or flies and grounders. Every kid got a hundred times at bat a day.

The pool opened at one. All afternoon we swam. A dime to get in. If you didn't have a dime, B. C. Crowell would let you in, anyway. We'd play Marco Polo, sharks and minnows, and dive from the high board. We'd come out at supper time looking like prunes.

In the evening we'd get together and play chase, tag out of jail, freeze tag, or just catch lightning bugs. Sometime during the week we'd try to collect enough Coca Cola bottles to trade in for movie money for Saturday.

We walked everywhere we went and every adult in our community watched out for every child. Slip off to the river to go fishing and your mama would know about it before you got home.

The only activity involving grown-ups was Vacation Bible School. They provided the glue and construction paper and popsickle sticks and read us the red words out of the Bible. You didn't register. You just showed up. If they ran out of cookies or Kool Aid, they would just make more.

We didn't stay inside and watch television and we didn't have Nintendo or Gameboys or the internet. Gee. Aren't we all glad our children won't be as deprived this summer as we once were?

Too Much Television for Kids is Not a New Concept

Shortly after this column was published we invested in a new satellite dish system. Now we have over 200 channels to choose from. Of course, according to my wife and kids, there is still nothing on.

There was much to do in all the newspapers recently concerning a study that claims children watch four and a half hours of television a day. At first I was aghast. "How terrible," I thought. I did what every respectable parent would do—I overreacted.

"Turn that mindless drivel off," I said to Jenna, my rising second grader, who was perched in her customary spot in the middle of the living room floor, eyes glued to a cartoon.

"What's drivel?" she responded.

"Never mind, " I said. "Turn off the television and go outside and play.

"It's still dark," she responded, "and pouring down rain." (We are early risers in the Huckaby household.)

I was not to be deterred from saving my child from the vast cultural wasteland. "Well turn off the television, anyway," I demanded.

Being the obedient child that she is, she turned off the television. An hour later I went looking for her and found her sitting at the computer. She was on the internet, in a "Kids Only" chatroom, talking to a third grader from Rochester, Minnesota with the screen name Spike.

"Come on Jenna," I said. Rug Rats cartoons are just starting. Make yourself at home in front of the television set and I'll fix some popcorn.

Do kids watch too much TV? Probably. But face it. Who can blame them? They have giant screens with surround sound and a hundred stations to choose from! My generation grew up with a small screen and the picture was, of course, black and white. We had three channels to choose from—2, 5, and 11-- and we were glued to the screen, too. We would sit and stare at a test pattern. If you're under the age of 47, go ask someone what a test pattern was.

Sociologists say our children are adversely affected by all the television they are watching, but I don't believe it makes as much of an impression on my kids as it did on me. Forty years from now, I bet they won't be able to name complete network lineups. I don't think they can name what they saw last week. But I remember almost every show, including the day of the week, time it came on and channel.

There were some great shows for kids. Remember Captain Kangaroo and Mr. Greenjeans? How about Buffalo Bob Smith and Howdy Doody? Every Atlantan of my generation, and that includes those of us in the Newton and Rockdale County hinterlands, grew up watching Officer Don and the Popeye Club. Anyone remember the contents of the goody bags in the treacherous game, ooey-gooey? Remember learning to count backward from 5 because that's how Officer Don started the cartoons? I ate tons of canned spinach, even though I hated the stuff, but never developed bulging biceps.

In addition to the Popeye Club, there was a kids show featuring a witch named Miss Boo, the Friday Night Shocker with Bestoink Dooley, and of course the Mickey Mouse Club. It was a must-see. The best part was the serials. Most of my buddies were partial to the Hardy Boys, but I liked Spin and Marty. I must admit, I probably watched the Mickey Mouse Club a while longer than most because I had begun to admire the way Annette Funicello filled out her Mousecateer sweater.

Saturday was great for television. Cartoons came on first, of course, and then a Tarzan movie, although when they showed one with someone other than Johnny Weismiller as Tarzan, I lost interest.

Roy Rogers, King of the Cowboys, came on on Saturdays. Roy had a sidekick named Pat Brady, who had a Jeep named Nellibelle. Pat Brady was always saying "mustard and custard!" when his Jeep wouldn't crank, which is as close as people came to cussin' on television in those days. When Trigger, Roy's Golden Palomino, died, Roy had him stuffed and he did the same to his dog, Bullet. I guess Roy's wife, Dale Evans, was a bit relieved that Roy went before she did.

Other Saturday favorites were Sky King ("Penny to Songbird, Penny to Songbird") and Fury—"The story of a horse, and the boy who loved him." They ended just in time to watch Dizzy Dean and Pee Wee Reese broadcast the Baseball Game of the Week, which happened to be between the New York Yankees and whoever they were playing. The game was never boring. The Falstaff Brewing Corporation was the sponsor of the Game of the Week and I do believe Dizzy Dean sampled the product as the game progressed. His commentary grew more and more colorful with every passing inning.

I'd say television made quite an impact on me. I could go on forever about the programs I watched on that old black and white set. In fact, I'd like to discuss the prime time schedule, but I don't have time. I've got to get on AOL and do a little research on a guy named Spike.

There She Was . . . Miss America

And now The Miss America Pageant--as we knew it--as
virtually disappeared. Is nothing sacred?

I confess. I watched the Miss America Pageant Saturday
night. I didn't watch the Florida—Tennessee game because both
of them couldn't lose. Besides, watching Miss America is a happy
link to my childhood.

We always watched Miss America. It was one of the high-
lights of the television season, ranking right up there with the Bob
Hope Christmas Show. Live from Atlantic City—The Miss
America Pageant.

I'm sure those of you who are Baby Boomers and older
did the same thing, even if you won't admit it. We'd sit and watch
the parade of states. Each contestant walked across the stage wearing a ribbon with her state name, sashayed up to the microphone,
and announced her name and the state she represented. "I'm Wendy
Wellbuilt and I'm Miss North Dakota!" It was a great geography
lesson. Hard evidence that there really is a North Dakota.

Burt Parks, who became associated with the pageant about
the time Arizona became a state, was always on hand. His wise-
cracks and small talk were intended to entertain the audience while
the girls changed clothes back stage. My daddy's favorite part of
the pageant was the swimsuit competition. I was about thirteen
before I realized why, which means that my son, Jackson, can
watch the show two more times. After that he stays upstairs and
watches Florida beat Tennessee.

My sister liked the evening gown competition and my
mother leaned toward the talent portion of the show. Her comments never varied from year to year.

"That Miss Mississippi sure can tap dance."

"I believe this year's Miss Texas can twirl a baton a whole
lot better than last year's."

"Miss New York sure does look natural with that dummy.
I can hardly see her mouth move."

I don't remember what other talents the contestants demonstrated back in the '50s, but I do recall that that the arts of ventriloquism, tap dancing, and baton twirling were always represented. I'm pretty sure I left the room when the ballerinas, classical pianists, and opera singers did their things.

After two or three hours, the accounting firm of Priceless and Icehouse would narrow the field and those whose beehives had not yet fallen would answer some antiseptic questions about whether women should be required to wear high heels and beads while they cooked supper and waited for Ward, Wally, and the Beaver. Finally, they would announce the winner. She would be given a crown, roses, and a fur coat. She always cried buckets as she paraded down the runway while Burt Parks sang "There she is, Miss America." I never understood why she was crying. Burt Parks didn't sing that bad. After her tearful walk, she was escorted to a big throne at the top of the stage. My whole family would always insist, for whatever reason, that the ugliest girl won and vow not to watch the next year. But we always did. So did the rest of the country. It was irresistible Americana.

The Miss America Pageant has gone through some rough times over the years. I think their troubles started when they dumped Burt Parks as a host because he was so old and hired Tarzan (actor Ron Ely) to take his place. They lost a lot of credibility with that move, as well as a lot of viewers who sat in on the show for purely nostalgic reasons.

They refused to pay royalties to the guy who wrote their theme song and for a couple of years weren't even allowed to have someone sing "There she is," even though there she was.

Vanessa Williams broke the color barrier, becoming the first African American Miss America, but had to give up her crown because Playboy Magazine revealed that she had had considerably more exposure than the pageant could bare, so to speak.

Other beauty pageants have stolen a little of Miss America's thunder. The Miss USA pageant, for instance, doesn't pretend to be about anything but flesh and beauty. That show is heavy into bikini swimsuits and there's not a tap dancer or baton twirler in sight.

A few years ago a debate came up as to whether to continue the swimsuit competition in the Miss America pageant. The pageant decided to let the people of America vote. Duh! The men voted that the swimsuits stayed by an overwhelming margin. That was like letting second graders vote on whether to have recess.

The swimsuit competition is still a bone of contention. This year's finalists were asked if they thought it was demeaning to women. Nine out of ten said that it was a great display of physical fitness. Right. I was watching that part of the program thinking, "I bet Miss South Carolina has a great resting heart rate." And Georgia Tech recruited Joe Hamilton because of his potential in calculus.

Now the pageant leadership is considering allowing divorced contestants as well as those who admit to having had an abortion. They would still ban contestants with children. What a concept. It's acceptable to have killed an unborn child but not to be a mother. "There she is ... our ideal?"

The times they are a changing. I wish we could change them back—to the days of Burt Parks and baton twirlers.

Old Man Winter Ain't What He Used to Be

The temperature dipped below freezing 17 straight days after this column appeared and we endured ice storms on successive weekends. I had to holler "calf-rope" and admit that Old Man Winter still had a frosty bite.

Is it just me, or is Old Man Winter losing a bit of his bite? Let's face it. Winter just ain't what it used to be. I don't pretend to be a scientist. I can't explain and do not fully understand the green house effect or the diminishing ozone layer or other factors that some say are causing global warming. I do, however, know this. It ain't as cold as it once was.

Winters were tough when I was a little boy. No, I'm not going to talk about how I walked four miles through the snow to get to school every day. It hardly ever snowed in Porterdale when I was little, and when it did, they closed school so we could stay outside and play in it. But I did walk to school, as did most of the other children in our town. It was only about a mile, not four. But I remember that being one cold mile in winter time.

The worst part of the walk to school was crossing the bridge over the Yellow River. I know why they have those signs, "Bridges ice before roadways." It was cold as a well diggers bottom going across that bridge in January and February. I still remember bundling myself up in my coat and hat. Remember those old leather caps, lined with fur? They had a little bitty bill and flaps that you could pull down over your ears. We did too, because if you didn't, your ears would feel like ice cubes and Nippy Harcrowe would sit behind you in class and thump them all morning. Nippy Harcrowe took great pleasure in thumping ears that had turned red from being ice cold.

I would start out every winter with a pair of gloves. The first one was always gone after about two days. That wasn't so bad because I could carry my books with one hand and put the other in my coat pocket. By the second week of winter, both gloves were long gone, which meant that by the time I got to school my hands were as red and frozen as my ears were when I couldn't find my cap.

Getting to school wasn't the only hardship created by the harsh winters I remember from my childhood. Bedtime created a set of problems all its own. Our four room mill house didn't have central heat. We had a gas space heater in the living room which kept that room and the kitchen fairly comfortable. There was no heat in the bedrooms. Of course, we never spent any time in the bedroom until it was time to go to bed. Then we crawled under several layers of homemade quilts and went to sleep, or tried to.

Sometimes it would be so cold that you'd resort to sleep-

ing in a stocking cap, or "sock hat" as we called it. The problem
with that was that the darn thing itched so much, you couldn't
stand to wear it. The windows would frost completely over and
sometimes there would be a thin layer of ice on the inside.

Heaven help you if you needed to go to the bathroom during the night. It was outside, on the back porch. Nothing in the
whole world could possibly be colder than bare feet on a linoleum
rug. You don't know cold if you haven't crawled out from under
a nest of quilts and stepped barefoot onto coldlinoleum.

I think winters were colder in general back in those days,
but occasionally we'd get a real cold snap and the temperature
would hover around zero degrees for a few days. That would
create real problems, because most of the houses, which were built
on brick pillars about four feet off the ground, were not under-
pinned. The cold air whipping under the houses would cause the
pipes to freeze and we'd be without water until the temperatures
began to rise. Of course, when they did begin to rise it created a
whole new problem. Frozen pipes usually burst. When the water
began to flow again it would flood the kitchen, causing my Daddy
to cuss and giving Oscar Harold Jackson, who was the plumber in
town, a lot of overtime.

To try and avoid frozen pipes, anytime Guy Sharp predicted that the Siberian Express, which is what he called a cold
front coming down from Canada, was on it's way, we would wrap
our pipes with newspaper and masking tape, catch up buckets of
water, and leave the faucet in the sink dripping, which was supposed to prevent the water in the pipes from freezing.

I don't know how often these cold snaps came through,
but I do remember that the river froze solid a couple of times
when I was little and having a wind burned face and chapped lips
was as much a part of life as stumped toes and bee stings were in
the summer.

Now, of course, we have it made. Our floors are carpeted
and warm and our pipes don't freeze. My kids hardly ever wear a
jacket because they never have to be outside long. The farthest
they have to go is a few feet, from the car to the house. I'm not

sure they even make those leather caps with the ear flaps anymore, and if they did, I know I couldn't make my boy wear one.

Be it global warming or changing life styles or whatever, winter isn't nearly as bad as it used to be. Most people are probably glad, but I sort of miss the cold weather. I think I'm going to watch the weather channel, and the next time the jet streams comes down toward us from over the North Pole, I'm going to leave my water dripping, just for old times sake.

My Apologies to Old Man Winter

The apology worked. We had an early spring.

A couple of weeks back I wrote what I intended to be a nostalgic and somewhat amusing look at the way winters used to be. In the column I suggested—all right—I came right out and said that Old Man Winter had lost a little bit of his bite. I bemoaned the fact that we hadn't had frozen precipitation in our little corner of the Southern world in a few years and even mentioned those two catch phrases "global warming" and "depletion of the ozone layer."

Well, a world wide conference on Global Warming was canceled in Washington D.C. this week—because of ice and cold weather. You know, of course, what the past two weekends have brought us, weather wise. But honest, it wasn't my fault!

It's amazing where people will place blame. I got dirty looks everywhere I went this week. I'm used to being abused and ignored by my wife and kids. I'm a husband and a father. It comes with the territory. But this week, total strangers have fixed me with stares icier than the pine trees that crashed onto the power lines last Sunday.

I went to a store the other morning to stock up on supplies. I made the mistake of listening to the television weather guy who was predicting about a hundred inches of snow, followed by thirty more inches of sleet, topped off with freezing rain that would keep us inside until Easter. I searched high and low for stocking caps and gloves. Jenna Huckaby intended to build a snowman, don't you know, and I couldn't let her little hands get cold, could I?

I couldn't find any caps or gloves. I finally asked a supposedly helpful sales associate in a bright red smock if she could help me locate the items I needed. She looked at me like I had the plague. "We're sold out," she finally responded. Under her breath I heard her mutter, "Thanks to your stupid column."

Needless to say, I was perplexed, and had no idea what the lady meant by her statement.

That same morning, one of my co-workers came by my room. Her normally fluffy hair was stuck to the sides of her head, as if it hadn't been shampooed in a few days. Her response to my good morning greeting was to make a face at me and bark, "It might be if I hadn't been without power for the past three days." Under her breath I heard her mutter, "Thanks to your stupid column."

Later that afternoon I sat down at the lunch table, in my usual spot. Two people got up and moved to a different table.

"What's wrong with them?" I inquired of the only person who chose to stay and have lunch with me.

"They are cold!" she replied, and then added, "Thanks to your stupid column."

Before I could remark, another lady approached us and said, "My husband said to tell you not to write any more columns about how mild the winters have become. He said you jinxed the weather."

I couldn't believe what I was hearing. All these people were blaming my column for the winter weather we've been having. As if I had any influence over anything. I can't even get our cat to go outside to use the litter box or my wife to make a sweet potato pie. I sure can't control the weather.

I wish I could influence world events by what I write. That would be better than having Aladin's lamp. All I'd have to do is write something and the opposite would happen. The first thing I'd write about is what a great recruiting class Georgia Tech is going to sign next week. Then I could just sit back and watch all those giant linemen and stud hoss defensive backs defect to other schools.

I think my next column would be about how money is the root of all evil and how glad I am that I'm not burdened with having any. Think how the green stuff would roll in if I wrote that!

This is kind of fun. It makes me dizzy thinking about all the things I could say! I could write about how glad I am the Braves haven't been able to win the World Series the last few years. I could write about how much I enjoy sitting in traffic on 138. I could even write about how glad I am we have smoking sections in restaurants, so I get the advantage of breathing polluted, cancerous air without having to buy cigarettes myself.

Get it? All the opposite things would happen and we'd have more World Championships, less traffic, and smoke free restaurants.

Trust me readers. My column has nothing to do with our recent blasts of winter weather. Just to prove it, I'm going to give you a preview of next week's column.

Say, you remember how it used to be back in the 1970's? Every now and then we'd have trees and even whole houses flattened by tornadoes. Wonder why we never have tornadoes anymore?

Just kidding. I wouldn't really do that. And just in case Old Man Winter really does subscribe to the Citizen— "Calf- rope! We give up! Go back to Buffalo—pretty please?"

High Prices at the Pump
are Giving Me Gas

And I thought prices were high in 1999. This was obviously written prior to the post-Katrina winter of 2006.

It's finally time to talk about gas. Not the kind you get at the all-you-can-stand-to-eat Mexican buffet, but the kind we were paying about 78 cents a gallon for last year which now is going for $1.39.

The joy of buying gas has been on the decline for years. I'm sure most of you remember the good old days when service stations—"fillin' stations" in Porterdale terminology—really offered service. I'm fully convinced that future historians will write that the decline of Western civilization started with self-service gasoline pumps.

We went from being met at the car with offers to "fill 'er up?" and "check that oil for ya?" to getting out of the car and doing it ourselves, but at least we got to go inside the store and pay a human being. Now we don't even get to do that. We just swipe a piece of plastic through a magnetic gizmo and pump away. (Am I the only one who has trouble figuring out which way the card should face?)

Last summer I drove from Conyers to Maine and back—nearly 3000 miles. I bought over 200 gallons of gasoline and never handed my money, or my credit card, to a human being. I did go inside one establishment to ask for directions. It was a waste of time. The guy behind the counter didn't speak English. Even if he had, something tells me he wouldn't have been able to distinguish Bar Harbor from a bar of soap. I wasn't from around there but he was from a whole lot farther away than I was.

Y'all remember how it used to be. You'd drive up to a gasoline pump and a guy with his name sewn across his pocket in cursive letters and a rag hanging from his belt would greet you at your car window. "Reg'lar or ethyl?" he might ask.

My daddy used to tell a story about a guy who was real

cheap but wanted people to think he was a big spender. He'd always tell the attendant to fill it up with hi-test while holding one finger outside the car window, indicating he wanted a dollar's worth.

Besides pumping your gas for you, the friendly fillin' station attendant would check your oil, wash your windshield, tug on your fan belt to make sure it wasn't about to snap, check the air pressure in your tires, and change the baby's diaper. He did all this while you sat right there in your car, if you so chose. If you wanted to stretch your legs, you could get out and buy a pack of peanuts and a bottled Coke. Everyone knows, of course, that a true Southerner poured the peanuts into the Coke before consuming them.

You got all of this service and then you paid about a quarter a gallon for your gas.

Sometimes stations would declare "Gas Wars." Ask a young person of today about a gas war and they are likely to recall Desert Storm. These weren't that kind of war. The way it worked was that one station decided it could get a few more customers if it sold gas for, say 28.9 instead of 29.9. Pretty soon the station on the other corner would drop down to 27.9 and so forth. Before you knew it, stations were practically giving gas away. Of course, with those big ol' 440 cubic inch gas guzzling engines we had back then, we wasted lots more money riding around town looking for the cheapest gas than we actually saved by buying it.

When folks had dropped prices as low as they possibly could, they started using other gimmicks to entice you to fill up at their place. One station gave away dishes. They were supposed to be something called Melmac, which isn't exactly fine China, but still sounds better than plastic, which is what they really were. Another gave away "Tenna Toppers," which were orange Styrofoam balls. The idea was to place them on top of your radio antenna, making it easier to locate your car in a parking lot. The problem was, this turned out to be a very successful promotion and it was almost impossible to find your car because everybody had a 'Tenna Topper.

My favorite gimmick was at the Gulf Station. They rigged up a hose which, when you drove over it, would trigger a big clock on the front of the station. The clock had a sweep hand with a little Gulf man on the end of it. It took ten seconds for the little Gulf man to travel around the face of the clock. If you weren't met by a smiling Gulf attendant by the time the Gulf man made it around the clock, your fill-up was free.

Every Friday and Saturday night my buddies and I, while cruising around town, would drive over to the Gulf station every fifteen or twenty minutes. We'd pull up to the pump, triggering the Gulf man on the clock and forcing Shorty Simpson, who was as wide as he was tall, to put down his Playboy magazine, tug on his pants, and run out toward the pumps. Shorty would arrive, out of breath, at our car window at about the same time the man on the clock reached 10. Naturally, we would drive away.

Eventually Shorty would say to heck with it and just sit there when we drove up, drooling over Miss May. Then, of course, we would sit there. What a great trick. We got free gas and got to hear Shorty cuss. Shorty knew more cuss words than anyone else in town.

Like so many other things, gas wars are probably gone for good. It's just as well. If we started saving too much money on gas the government would probably just confiscate it. Besides, who needs a 'Tenna Topper, anyway?

What We All Need is More Time on the Front Porch

I still haven't been back to sit on my friends' front porch, but it's still on my list of things to do.

I had to visit some folks the other day to pick up something I needed. Actually, we didn't get to visit. Nobody visits anymore. We're much too busy. I just dashed in and dashed out.

I wish I could have stayed, because they had a great front porch. It was big enough for five rocking chairs, arranged in a semicircle so folks could actually look at one another while they talked. It faced the east so if people had been sitting and rocking and conversing, they would have been warmed by the morning sun. It was also covered, to provide shade during the heat of the day.

What I wouldn't have given to have been able to sit a spell, rocking and talking and enjoying the fine spring day. But I had deadlines to meet and places to be. I was much too busy to waste time sitting on a front porch.

Isn't that a pity?

We have all gotten too busy to sit on the front porch. Most new houses don't even have one. We have a small one and even have a couple of rocking chairs on it, but about the only time I ever actually sit and rock is in the summer months when I carry my coffee and my newspaper out there and enjoy a few moments solitude.

The house I grew up in, in Porterdale, had a great front porch. It went all the way across the front of the house. Half of it was "screened in" and half wasn't. It had a swing big enough for three people and several rocking chairs.

We spent a lot of time on our front porch. In the fifties and early sixties Highway 81, through Porterdale, was one of the busiest in the state, especially at shift changing time. I used to sit on the front porch swing, watching cars go by for hours at a time. My sister and I would play a little game. We'd each pick a color and get points for each car that passed that was the color we had picked. She always won, but I didn't care. It was something to do.

During the hot summer months we'd sit on the porch in the evening, when the air had begun to cool just a bit, and shell peas and butter beans and pull the husks off fresh corn. My mama would fill two freezers with fresh garden vegetables every summer, all of which were either shelled or shucked on the front porch. They would last almost all winter, too. When I'd get tired of shelling or shucking, mama would tell me to take a break and chase the lightning bugs that always flittered around the bushes in front of the porch.

Porterdale had sidewalks. That's another thing we don't have enough of these days. People used to walk up and down them, too, giving other folks a chance to invite them up to sit and talk. And folks did. Sitting on a front porch talking to people is a whole lot better way to spend an evening than sitting in front of a television set watching someone try to win a million dollars.

When I got a little older, I would sit on the front porch late at night, watching for my daddy to come home from the second shift at the mill. I could tell his headlights from all the other cars in town and as soon as I saw them come up the hill toward our house I'd hurry through the house to meet him. A thirty minute talk before bedtime was better than not seeing him at all.

When I became a high school front porch sitter I quit noticing the colors of the cars that passed our house and started noticing the drivers, especially when they were young and female. When I was in the ninth grade, Sheila Bates, who was homecoming queen and captain of the varsity cheerleaders, rode by our house in a convertible with the top down. She saw me sitting on the porch and honked her horn and waved at me. I sat there for hours watching for her to come back by, but she never did.

Not too many years later I learned that there were better things to do while sitting on a front porch swing on a hot August night than shell peas. My daughter will be in high school soon. Maybe it's a good thing our porch isn't big enough for a swing, after all.

When I went away to college, one of the things I missed most, other than my mama's cornbread and fried chicken, was the time we used to spend on the front porch. The person who coined the phrase "quality time" probably had front porch sitting in mind.

The day of my daddy's funeral, twelve years ago, I sat in that same front porch swing and wondered if life would ever be the same again. A cotton farmer from Mansfield sat beside me, saying nothing. I doubt if I ever told him how much having him there helped that day.

My mama died last December and we sold her house. I rode by it the other day and there were kids' toys all over the front porch. That made me smile. I hope they find as much happiness on that front porch as I did.

I think I'm going to spend more time on my own front porch this spring. Who knows. Maybe I'll even go back to the house I visited the other day and invite myself to sit in the shade with the people who live there while we rock and solve the problems of the world.

Well, I might.

It's a Grand old Flag...
and long may it wave!

It's a Grand Old Flag . . .
and long may it wave!

Patriotism. Now there's a word that seems to have gone out of style.

In my opinion, which is the only one I ever express, we don't do a good enough job impressing upon our children the importance of those who have fought and died to make our country the greatest on earth, which I am fully convinced it is.

The flag has become more of a decoration than a symbol of freedom and the *Star Spangled Banner* is something we sing before ball games.

Our country was founded by honorable men who believed in an ideal and were willing to risk their lives so that other people could live in a land of liberty. Down through the generations, others have had to leave home and take up the cause of Freedom around the globe.

These people were special. We owe them much more than a short chapter in this book. For now, at least, a short chapter in this book is all I can offer. That and a word of thanks for protecting our grand old flag and a prayer that it may forever wave over "the land of the free and the home of the brave."

Remembering the Regular Guys

This column first appeared in the Atlanta Journal-Constitution on Memorial Day in 1997. Tony Piper's name is still on that black marble wall.

My daughter, Jamie Leigh, is going to Washington this week with her fifth-grade class from Sims Elementary School in Conyers. I hope her teachers don't mind, but I asked my daughter to look up an old high school buddy for me while she's there. I showed her his picture in mv class yearbook and told her where to find him.

My buddy's name is Tony Piper. I haven't seen him since the night in early June when we graduated from Newton County High School. That was 27 years ago. It seems like a week. Tony and I weren't the best of friends. We didn't really run together, But we were pals. We had classes together and cut up together. In P.E. one day, my elbow caught his mouth. His tooth was chipped and his mouth bled right through English and world history. For two years, he good-naturedly threatened to get me back.

Tony wasn't an honor graduate. He wasn't on any athletic teams or in the band. He was just a regular guy. He was a little shorter than average and well put together, with curly black hair, bright brown eyes and a swarthy complexion. He would have made a great pirate.

The last time I saw Tony, he was loading a cooler of beer into the trunk of a friend's Camaro. He and about half of our newly graduated class were heading to Daytona Beach. We shook hands and slapped each other on the back. I warned him about what not to do at the beach. He grinned and promised that he'd try his darndest to do all the things I had warned him against.

I've never forgotten Tony's grin. He had never bothered to have the tooth repaired that I chipped. We promised to get together over the summer and keep in touch, and all those other things graduating seniors promise each other, but he never did.

That fall, I left my home in Porterdale to begin my education at the University of Georgia. Tony got drafted and began his education at Fort Benning.

As I said, I never saw Tony after we graduated, but I'm having my daughter look him up, just like I do whenever I'm in Washington. He's easy to find. He's just a little northeast of the Lincoln Memorial. He's Section 3 West, Line 119 on a black marble wall.

He shares that wall with almost 60,000 other regular guys who were asked to do something for their country. Tony's war wasn't one of your popular wars—like World War II or Desert Storm. His war was politically incorrect. But I had Civics and U.S. Government with Tony—trust me, he wasn't aware of the politics. He swore an oath to defend the United States of America and I'm sure he felt that if his fighting in the jungles of Southeast Asia wasn't necessary to the defense of his country, his leaders wouldn't have sent him there.

As a history teacher, I struggle each day with finding ways to help young people realize that the freedom they take so much for granted was not free, but was purchased at a terrible cost. About a million and a half regular guys, like Tony Piper, have paid the ultimate price. Tony paid it on July 31, 1971. Fourteen months after Daytona Beach.

Memorial Day is supposed to be the day we say thanks to those who have made that supreme sacrifice. I hope we can pause long enough today--during our cookouts and fish fries and pool parties—to remember why we're having a holiday.

And I hope that an 11-year-old girl can rub her fingers across a name on a wall and understand—just a little— what her daddy's old friend was asked to give on her behalf. I hope we all can.

Conceived in Blood . . . Born of Words
Happy Birthday USA

I respectfully dedicate this column to all the brave men and women who have served in the Armed Forces of our country. Thanks.

It was early summer in Philadelphia, PA. Trust me. Georgia ain't got nothing on Philadelphia when it comes to heat in July. The day I was there was the hottest in the history of the weather bureau. You can look it up. 105 degrees in the shade, if there had been any shade. I was there with my wife, Lisa, and our daughter Jamie, who was still in a stroller. We were waiting in a long, long line to get inside Independence Hall and see where the Declaration of Independence had been signed. A kid came by with a cooler on a little red wagon, selling Cokes for two dollars a piece. It was the best money I spent on the trip. We finally got inside to view the place where the world had been changed in 1776. It was worth the wait.

Here's why we stood in the heat for two hours to see inside an old building. England had set up about a dozen colonies in what they called the "New World" in order to help the British economy. You know—raise raw materials themselves. Buy low. Sell high. Not much different than today. The system worked out pretty well, too. They had a good thing going. Then old King George III got greedy.

One thing led to another—unfair taxes, high tariffs, unrealistic trade restrictions. The colonists soon realized that they didn't even have the rights that their fellow Englishmen across the pond enjoyed. A few radicals like Thomas Payne, John Hancock, Patrick Henry, and Samuel Adams began stirring up the masses. More stuff happened. The Boston Tea Party. More harsh laws. More strong words.

Words. The revolution began with words. Words put together in such a way as to cause people to think about the human condition. Words spoken with eloquence and passion that stirred the emotions of a people and drove them beyond words and ideals. Words which caused people to decide that principles such as liberty and freedom were more important than security and safety.

"Give me liberty or give me death." Seven words.

"Taxation without representation." Three words.

"If they mean to have a war, let it begin here." Eleven words.

Words turned to action. On a cold April morning a group of farmers stood on a village green and faced the strongest army in the world. The British regulars fired into the crowd of farmers and the farmers fled. Seven miles down the road they would not flee, however. They would return fire upon the British, time and time again, chasing the invaders all the way back to Boston town.

Twelve months later, the finest this new land had to offer met right there in Philadelphia, in the building we waited in the heat to see. The birthplace of our country. These weren't poor, downtrodden citizens who had nothing to lose. These were the most successful men in the colonies. They had prospered under British rule. They met throughout the long hot summer of '76 and debated principles with little or no thought of their own best interests. I wonder if the world ever witnessed such a gathering of wisdom and honor in one place, before or since.

Red haired Thomas Jefferson, who would pen the document that they finally agreed to sign. Benjamin Franklin, author, inventor, and entrepreneur, whose wit and wisdom held the convention together more than once.

"We must all hang together, or surely we shall all hang separately." Twelve words.

John Hancock, who signed the document in letters so big that King George III could read it without his spectacles. Georgia's own Button Gwinnett, who would die in a duel of honor before a year passed. Richard Henry Lee, whose grandson would fight on a far different field of honor. Samuel Adams. John Adams. Fifty-seven men in all pledged their lives, fortunes, and sacred honor to an idea; an idea based on a basic statement of human rights.

"We hold these truths to be self-evident: that all men are created equal, that they are endowed by their Creator with certain unalienable rights, that among these are life, liberty, and the pursuit of happiness." Thirty-five words.

By signing the Declaration of Independence, these men were signing a death warrant, if their revolution failed. It did not. Many of the signers did lose their lives. Many lost their fortunes, but not one lost the honor which they saw as sacred.

Thus on July 4, 1776, our country, the United States of America, which had been conceived in the blood of Lexington and Concord, was born. Born with words as her midwife. Words, yes. But words backed up by a noble people who have paid a tremendous price to see that the honor of our founding fathers has been upheld throughout the generations.

Celebrate this weekend. Enjoy barbecues and fish frys and family gatherings. Visit the lake or the pool or the beach or the mountains or the neighbor's back yard. Watch the parade or run in the Peachtree Roadrace or do any of the things Americans do to celebrate our birthday. But remember. Please take time to remember. Our freedom has never been free and never will be. We've been given a wonderful legacy. We must all be ever-vigilant if we want to pass it on to the next generation.

Happy Birthday, USA.

We Run into Heroes in the
Most Unlikely Places

Mr. Pinkerton is now dead and gone--but he will never be forgotten--at least not by me.

An old man sat in front of me at last week's high school football game. I'm a sucker for old men, especially when they wear houndstooth hats. My daddy used to be an old man and often wore a houndstooth hat. I hope the gentleman who sat in front of me doesn't mind being called old, but he is. He told me so himself. He is 83. That's pretty old.

Personally, I've never understood why people object to being old. It sure beats the alternative.

But back to the gentleman who sat in front of me at the game. He and his family had been sitting right behind the student cheering section. When they realized that the students were not just standing for the kickoff, but rather the whole game, my new friend and his family began to search for higher ground. They wound up in front of me.

I watched my new friend throughout the first half. He sat beside his wife and, I learned, his daughter. He leaned on a beautiful hand carved cane and didn't say much. He paid closer attention to the band at halftime than he had to the game. During the second half he turned around and made a comment to me about the Braves jacket I was wearing. It was finally football weather last Friday night.

Seeing my jacket inspired him to relate an interesting tidbit about his past. When he was in the army, back in '44, he had a driver for his jeep. Turns out his driver would go on to play baseball in the big leagues and would eventually wind up as a coach for the Braves. I guess the connection was that my new friend's jeep driver wore a coat like mine to work.

I had an option here. I could nod politely and say "uh huh," or I could reply with a question or comment of my own. In addition to being a sucker for old men, I'm also a sucker for men who served in the armed forces during the '40s. The army was pretty busy back then, you know. I asked him if he had served overseas. That was all I needed to say. He was off and running.

I learned that the gentleman in the hounds1tooth hat had, indeed, served overseas. He was in North Africa first. Later he was sent to fight his way across Italy. He was part of the largest invasion in the history of the world and landed in France around the first of August in 1944. That's three weeks after D-Day. He fought his way across France and had made it all the way to the Rhine River by the time Germany surrendered. Upon his return to the States after WW II he joined the Alabama National Guard. Wouldn't you know it? They were Federalized and he got another all expense paid trip overseas. This time he went to Korea. Korea was just as unpleasant a place to visit in the early '50s as France had been in the '40s.

I learned a lot more about Mr. Pinkerton, which is my new friend's name. I learned that he graduated from the University of Alabama and also attended Auburn and UGA. I learned that he had been a teacher and a school principal and I learned that I had, in fact, taught his granddaughter. She was part of the Heritage band's flag corps, thus the rapt attention to the halftime show.

I was very glad that I had worn my Braves jacket to the game, thus giving Mr. Pinkerton a reason to strike up a conversation with me. I was reminded, once again, that a huge number of the old men we run into and take for granted every day are not just old men. They are heroes. They left the safety and security of this country, said goodbye to mamas and daddies and wives and children and friends and sweethearts and left home for the duration. They fought Hitler and Tojo and won. They saved the world. They really did. They saved the world.

Then they returned home and helped build this country into the greatest industrial power in the history of the world. They made sure that their children were the best educated generation with the most opportunity in the history of our republic.

Look around you. Those old men you see in fast food restaurants and stand behind in line at Wal Mart are not just old men. Take time to talk to them. Find out their stories. Tell them thank you. We're about to head into a new century and pretty soon all the heroes that preserved our society will be gone. Then we won't be able to thank them, or hear their stories. Or learn from them.

During our conversation Mr. Pinkerton expressed dismay that November 11, Veteran's Day, is all but ignored in this country. I agree. We should pay more attention to that day. But I also don't think we should wait until Veterans Day to thank the Mr. Pinkerton's of the world. They deserve our gratitude every day and for some of them November 11 might be too late. As for me, five weeks before Veterans Day, I'd like to say, "God bless all the Mr. Pinkertons, and God bless America."

12
Just Stuff

Just Stuff

Everywhere I go these days, I seem to run into people who read my column, and they all seem to have questions. The most often asked question, other than, "How much do you get payed?" is "How long does it take you to write your column ?"

That, of course, varies from day to day.

The next most popular question is, "Where do you get all your ideas for columns?"

That is a good question. A lot of my column ideas come from my memory, of course. I often write about my childhood in Porterdale. Sometimes I write about my family and other times about the people I meet at work or at play.

Sometimes, I must admit, I really struggle for a topic. I often sit down at my desk and place my fingers on the keyboard of my word processor without a clue as to what my subject will turn out to be. So far I've been lucky. I've never drawn a complete blank.

The columns in this chapter didn't seem to fit into any neat little category. They are a hodge podge on a wide variety of subjects. Some of them, however, are among my favorites. I hope you'll like them, too.

The Times They Are a'changin' at UGA

The young lady about whom this column was written did, indeed, graduate from UGA. She now works in Houstin, texas--and she's still one of Georgia's finest, and one of my all-time favorite people.

There are a thousand better things to do on a Sunday afternoon in spring than sit inside writing a paper for English 101. But I've known Stephanie since she was in diapers and she is so sweet and has those beautiful brown eyes and besides that, her uncle was best man at my wedding, so how could I say no?

It was really sort of fun. I got to help write about Mickey Mantle. I'm sure this precious child wasn't born the last time Mantle homered in Yankee Stadium, but she wrote about him, nonetheless. After we'd finished the assignment, she questioned me about the "good old days" at UGA—back when her uncle and I were freshmen. She was wondering if things had changed much. I believe they have.

For one thing, it takes about a 1200 on the SAT to qualify for admission. Two of us used to get in for that. For another thing, the Fifth Quarter is long gone and so is Bob Poss' Restaurant. What I wouldn't give for one of his barbecued pork pig sandwiches—or a BP special, which was a chargrilled hamburger steak with melted cheese and grilled onions on top. It was served with hush puppies by a lady with a gold tooth who was at least a hundred years old.

And Dean Tate doesn't stand outside the coliseum in his red baseball cap holding a bullhorn to direct registration. Students register over the internet now, from the comfort of their own homes. What sissies! How will they learn toughness if they never have to figure out how to sneak into registration early or push and shove to get the last class card for the only easy professor in the biology department. Dean Tate would roll over in his grave if he knew about electronic registration.

I believe the students are much more sophisticated than we were thirty years ago. Thirty years? How could it be possible? That Latin guy who said "Time flies" was right on the money. It was almost three decades ago when I entered the great and wonderful University of Georgia. I can't remember what I had for lunch yesterday, but every moment of my first week in Athens is crystal clear. I must have walked a hundred miles because I wasn't sure which bus to ride. It was 102 degrees every day, but I sweltered in long sleeve button down shirts because I wanted to impress the coeds by looking collegiate.

I know I was the most naive of my five thousand classmates, and the most homesick. Oz wasn't nearly as different from Kansas as UGA was from Porterdale. I lived in a dorm with more Yankees than Sherman brought with him. Talk about culture shock! They could have been from Mars and Neptune instead of Pittsburgh and Brooklyn. I was the only freshman on my hall and the upper classmen all made fun of the way I looked and the way I dressed and, especially, the way I talked. They also sent me out after curfew every night on Waffle House runs. I never got caught, but I gained twenty-five pounds my first quarter.

I didn't tell Stephanie much about what her uncle and I did in college. The statute of limitations hasn't expired on some of the stuff and some of it was just too stupid to admit, but there were a few moments worth savoring, which I shared with my tutoree.

I told her about her uncle's roommate stealing a hat right off a policemen's head the night before the 1972 Auburn game. He snatched it and ran like the wind. The policeman was Kent Lawrence who, at that time, was probably the fastest man who had ever played football at UGA. Our buddy was caught, tackled, and headed for jail after three steps. Kent Lawrence was not just a good cop, he was a good guy. After our friend had been bailed out, his arresting officer came by the dorm to make sure he was all right and stayed long into the night. Auburn and Pat Sullivan won the game the next day.

I also told her about the Streaking Phenomena. During

one unbelievable week there were people all over campus running, walking, being pushed in wheelchairs, riding horseback, ala
Lady Godiva, and even jumping out of airplanes—all naked as
jay birds. One night over 1200 students disrobed and walked a
mile across campus, filing two by two into Sanford Stadium in an
attempt to break the "world streaking record." She really wanted
to know if her uncle and I participated, but I refused to answer.
Our Founding Fathers didn't think up the fifth amendment for
nothing.

I could have reminisced forever, but there was work to be
done. Maybe she'll come back one day soon.

One thing hasn't changed at UGA. The Freshman English teachers are still brutal graders. We only got a B on our
Mickey Mantle paper. Next time I'll tell Stephanie we should write
about Herschel Walker.

Wedding Bells Are Ringing

*I finally was able to retire from the wedding photography
business. Now the only time I cry on Saturday afternoon's
is when my wife hands me the list of chores she has lined
up for me to do.*

It's spring. The dogwoods have bloomed, pollen has
turned our entire city yellow, Freaknik has come and, thankfully,
gone, and wedding bells are ringing. Young men's thoughts may
turn to baseball in the spring, but young women's thoughts turn to
marriage.

I didn't know what true happiness was until I got married. Of course, by then it was too late. (Just kidding. Honest!)

I go to a lot of weddings. Twenty-five or thirty a year.
Over two hundred in the '90s. Before you ask, no, I'm not a glut-
ton for punishment, nor do I have an unusual addiction to dry

cake and punch. I get paid to go to weddings. At least I get paid to photograph weddings.

I became a wedding photographer quite by accident. Someone was getting married at the last minute and needed pictures. I had a camera. One thing led to another. Now I spend over half the Saturdays in the year saying, "Big smile! Don't blink!" I've yet to ask someone to say cheese.

Unusual thinks happen at weddings. Some are downright funny, or would be if the participants weren't so stressed out. A person's wedding day should be the happiest day of his or her life, but few people allow themselves to enjoy it. Most are too busy worrying that their perfect day will lack perfection.

I once photographed a wedding involving a four year old child. He was the ring bearer. He had trouble standing still at the alter. Imagine that. You dress a four year old boy up in a tuxedo, give him a white satin pillow to hold, ask him to pose patiently for pictures and be kissed on the cheek by a four year old flower girl, and then expect him to stand still for thirty minutes on a Saturday afternoon in front of two hundred people. How thoughtless of him not to cooperate.

The groom was disturbed by the child's behavior at the alter and as he and his bride were making their way up the aisle, after the ceremony, he began to complain. By the time the newlyweds got outside the church they were shouting at one another. The groom got into his rented convertible and drove away in a huff, leaving the bride to attend the reception alone. Luckily I got paid in advance.

I was shooting a wedding, in another state, which involved a groom who was a Marine Corps pilot. The night before the wedding he and his buddies went out on the town for a final fling. I'm not sure, but I think they visited establishments that featured adult entertainment. I'm fairly certain alcoholic beverages were involved. The Marines got into an argument, which turned into a brawl. I don't know what the other guys looked like, but the groom could only have one side of his face photographed. The bride was not amused. Just a guess, but I'd be willing to bet the honeymoon was less pleasant for the groom than it might have been.

One nervous young groom arrived at the church without the wedding ring. By the time he discovered his mistake he didn't have time to send for it. I loaned him mine for the service. He wore it on his honeymoon and lost it in the ocean. Or so he said. My wife was about as amused as the bride of the Marine.

One bride got cold feet and canceled on the very morning of the wedding. I did photograph a wedding for her, exactly 52 Saturdays later. The groom was different. Even though I've only been in business ten years, I've had several repeat customers. One person claimed the trifecta and has booked me for all three of her weddings. Nothing like satisfied customers.

I've seen wedding cakes collapse, attendants faint, and one poor bride dropped lipstick on the front of her dress, leaving a red streak six inches long. I learned from that experience that hairspray, nail polish remover, and Clorox are worthless at getting lipstick out of white satin. Whiteout and spray paint don't do much for fabric, either.

Most weddings are in the afternoon or evenings which always reminds me of a quote by Joe Willie Namath. He once advised, "Never get married in the morning. You don't know who you might meet that afternoon."

However, I'm a romantic at heart and despite the divorce rate and the odds against long unions, I always get sentimental when I watch the newlyweds exchange vows. I find myself hoping that all couples will feel like Mr. T. K. Adams. Mr. Adams was band director at Cousins Middle School when I was a rookie teacher and he took me under his wing. He remains one of the wisest men I've ever known. He told me many times, "The only regret I have about marriage is that I wasn't born married."

Me too. And to all the spring couples—Happy Honeymoon.

Driving a Stick Shift Isn't All it's Cracked Up to Be

As this book went to press my oldest child, Jamie, was only half a year away from being old enough for a learner's permit. I wonder if buying her a straight shift car would deter her from driving?

While driving through Olde Town the other morning, I encountered a traffic jam. As I approached Milstead Avenue, I saw what I assumed was the reason, and it was a peculiar sight. A gray haired man in a business suit was standing in the middle of the road, seemingly carrying on a conversation with a black Jeep Wrangler. I must admit that my first reaction was, "What a place to carry on a conversation!" As my lane began to move and I got closer to the situation I couldn't help but laugh.

Behind the wheel of the Wrangler was a teenaged girl who was obviously having her first intimate encounter with a straight shift and a hill. The gray haired gentleman was trying to explain the finer points of the brake, the accelerator, and the clutch. I'm sure the young lady was wondering why automakers would place three pedals in a car to be used by a person with only two feet. She was also thinking, I bet, that driving a straight shift wasn't nearly as much fun as it looked.

As I passed the unfortunate driver, a long line of very patient motorists had formed behind her. She was alternately lurching forward a few inches, choking down, cranking her car, and lurching forward a few more inches. Tears of frustration were running down her cheeks. As the late Tennessee Ernie Ford would have said, "Bless her little pea pickin' heart."

While I completed my errands, my mind began to wander. For a brief while I was sixteen again, driving to a Braves' game in an Opal Kadet with four on the floor. That car was a cruel trick foreign automakers played on General Motors. I was, for the first time, venturing outside the borders of Newton County behind the wheel of that car. As if that weren't adventure enough, I was with a date. Amazingly, I arrived at the Atlanta Stadium parking lot without incident. It was leaving the game when my problems started.

All 40,000 spectators were trying to leave the parking lot at the same time by way of the same exit. I headed, instinctively, for low ground and the back of the parking lot. The policeman directing traffic turned me around and made me follow the crowd, right toward a very steep hill. Thinking back on the incident, I'm certain he knew I was in a car I couldn't drive and with a girl I wanted desperately to impress. As fate would have it, the line of traffic came to a complete standstill just as I reached the steepest part of the hill. Naturally, as I tried to let out the clutch, very carefully, so as not to run into the car in front of me, I choked down.

No problem. Could happen to anybody.

I cranked the car and tried again. Same results.

Over and over and over. We cranked. We lurched. We choked down.

By now sweat is pouring from my body. I am beyond embarrassed. To make matters worse, the people leaving the ball game were not nearly as patient as those folks in Conyers last week. They began to blow their horns and scream at me. The sadistic cop who had sent me up the hill in the first place added insult to injury by shouting at me to get my junk heap out of the way.

My date, to her credit, didn't laugh or make fun of me— at least not then. In fact, she offered to help by mashing the gas while I controlled the brake and the clutch. Her efforts were futile and having her leg on my side of the console made me even more nervous than trying to drive the car.

Finally, in desperation, I inched my way into a U-Turn, in direct violation of Officer Sadist, and headed toward the back of the parking lot. Downhill I could do. We were going in the wrong direction, but at least we were going.

We drove in slow circles around the Atlanta Stadium parking lot until all the cars had departed the scene. Then we eased our way up the dreaded hill, out of the parking lot and onto Capitol Avenue, where we promptly missed the turn which would have put us on I-20, headed home.

When I realized I had missed my turn I did what any another mortified 16 year-old would have done. I panicked and took the first available road. We were on I-85 South, headed toward the Atlanta Airport. We passed several exit ramps but I was afraid to get off on any of them because they were all so steep.

Thank heaven, we finally ran across I-285. Naturally we got on 285 headed in the wrong direction, but, "Hey. It's round." We finally got back to my date's house, a mere two hours after the baseball game had ended. Her father actually believed our story about why it took us two hours to make a thirty minute trip. I guess he had driven a stickshift, too, once upon a time.

To the young lady in the black Jeep Wrangler. Don't feel bad. We've all been there. Just remember, in the words of Billy Bob Fraley, first inductee into the Shade Tree Mechanic Hall of Fame, "If you can't find them, grind them." And trust me, driving a stick shift won't be the last thing you do that looks like more fun than it really is.

Buckle Up—It's Time for Class

I teach Social Studies now. It's not nearly so dangerous.

While sitting in traffic on 138 last week, I realized I was beside a Driver's Education car. Even before I saw the magnetic sign on top of the car I noticed the white knuckles and terrified expression of the person beside me. The driver looked a little nervous, too.

As traffic cleared I proceeded and soon left the student

driver behind, but my thoughts turned to other days when I might have been the uneasy instructor. I taught Driver's Education for a number of years in a variety of settings. It's not the most soothing way to make a living. In fact, I had more than my share of Maalox moments.

When I was in my mid-twenties I took temporary leave of my senses and accepted a teaching job in south Georgia. Trust me. Life is different below the gnat line. The people are among the nicest in the world, but the pace of life was not exactly Buckhead. I'm sure the slower tempo would appeal to me now, but was a tough adjustment for a single guy in the '70s.

One of my duties was to teach Driver's Education one period a day. The headmaster of the school assured me that it would be the easiest part of my schedule because all the kids in that rural community had grown up driving tractors and farm vehicles. Together the students and I learned that driving a car on city streets was much different than driving a tractor across a plowed field.

I should have known what to expect when on the first day of school one of my students-to-be, a senior cheerleader who had a driver's license and was taking the course to improve her insurance rates, drove her mother's car into a ditch on the way to school. Her father happened to be one of my best friends in the community and her mother was in the habit of feeding me fried chicken after church on Sunday. I helped the young lady out of the ditch. She was grateful, but the subsequent teasing at the hands of her family was unmerciful.

Anyone familiar with Driver's Ed knows that a certain number of hours are devoted to class discussion, book work, and the ever present videos that are designed to scare the dickens out of anyone who sees them. During one of my scintillating lectures about pedestrian safety I mentioned that in our urban communities a person gets hit by a car every 30 minutes. One overgrown boy in the back of the class, who might have been the only person still awake, slowly raised his hand.

Impressed that he wanted to respond, I called on him.

"Coach Huckaby," he said in a slow South Georgia drawl, "Somebody ought to tell that fool to stay on the sidewalk."

The same student was driving the Driver's Ed car through the streets of beautiful downtown Pelham one morning. I gave him instructions to turn right at the next traffic light, which happened to be green. He dutifully turned on his blinker and made a perfect stop at the green light.

"Go ahead," I encouraged him. "Make your turn."

He turned and smiled at me and said, in that same slow drawl, "You can't fool me, Coach Huckaby. The sign says 'turn right on red.'"

To my amazement, he sat there and waited until the light turned red, then looked both ways and made his turn. The young man drove with me the whole year without ever understanding about turning right on green as well as red. But he didn't run over any pedestrians, on or off the sidewalk. I'm not sure exactly what became of that student, but I'm fairly certain he's not in aerospace engineering.

My students and I had all sorts of adventures during the two years I spent in south Georgia. I enjoyed the excitement so much that I continued to teach the course when I returned to the Atlanta area. Driving with inexperienced teenagers on a country road is one thing. Driving on 285 is quite another.

I didn't know what life in the fast lane was all about until I let a group of students talk me into driving from College Park to the Varsity for lunch. Surprisingly, we negotiated the traffic and got there without incident. The problem came when it was time to leave the Varsity. If you've ever tried to cross three lanes of traffic and make a left turn onto North Avenue at noon on a given Friday, you understand what the fifteen year old girl whose turn it was to drive was going through. She finally picked what she thought was an opportune time and hit the gas. I guess she just assumed all the taxis heading toward her would stop. I've never heard so many screeching tires in my life. Nor have I been cursed in so many languages at once. I didn't understand what any of the drivers were saying, but the sign language was quite clear. Miraculously, everyone survived her takeoff unscathed, but that was our first and last trip to the Greasy V.

I taught Driver's Ed for several years after that and am firmly convinced that I'd have lots more hair and less gray in my beard if I had stuck to the academics. I haven't driven with a student in years and I'm very glad of that. In fact, any time I get disillusioned with my history classes, I can be very thankful that reading Shakespeare doesn't require a seat belt.

It's Diet Time Again

I actually did find a diet that worked and lost 35 pounds in less than two months. Then Christmas came . . . and the rest is history.

OK. This is it. This time I'm really going to do it. Yours truly is about to embark upon a very stringent diet—again. This time the weight is going to go away—and stay gone. Nothing to it. I'll burn more calories than I consume and in no time at all I'll be as slim and trim as I was back before my first child was born.

At the time my wife, Lisa, became pregnant for the first time I weighed about 160 pounds, compared to the 214 pounds I currently carry around with me. In the ensuing nine months we both gained fifty pounds. Hey, I wanted to be supportive! She ate for two—I ate for two. She wanted hot fudge cake at midnight. What kind of husband would let her eat alone? When she had cravings, I shared them. When she didn't have cravings, I had them for her. She got larger and so did I. She replaced her wardrobe with maternity clothes. I let my belt out another notch and started wearing my pants below my belly instead of around it.

She left most of her extra weight in the delivery room, except for the 10 pounds we brought home with us, wrapped in a pink blanket. I'm still trying to lose mine. Actually, I've been at it for quite a while. Our oldest child will be 14 in a month. I have tried dozens of times to lose weight with varying degrees of success. There are several reasons I have such a hard time with dieting.

One problem is, I have an image to maintain. Everybody who knows me knows that I pride myself on being a Southerner, and that the Southern male is expected to consume large quantities of fried chicken, ham, sausage, bacon, buttermilk biscuits, fried catfish, and, of course, barbecued pork and Brunswick stew. We have a heritage to maintain and never let it be said that I haven't done my part.

Another problem is that the calendar works against me when I try to lose weight. For instance, Jamie, the child with whom I got so large in the first place, was born in October. The first month of her life I couldn't really be expected to fall off any. Snacks and late night feedings go hand in hand and with friends and neighbors bringing food over and such, I actually put on another pound or two. But as soon as that month was over I was determined to start dropping pounds.

Wouldn't you know it? Right at the end of October— Halloween. Not wanting to disappoint the small ones in the neighborhood, I bought a large supply of Trick or Treat candy. It rained that year on Halloween. Somebody had to eat all those leftover Snickers and Butterfingers, and so it goes, year after year. Get the Halloween candy cleaned up and it is Thanksgiving. The very holiday developed around food. Thanksgiving leads right into December and the whole month is just one big Christmas party after another.

January is good for New Year's resolutions about weight loss, but realistically it just isn't feasible. You're expected to eat ham hocks and black eyed peas and cornbread on the first day of the year in order to assure good luck. By thirty minutes past noon my resolution to cut back on my eating is already shot.

Now television begins to work against me. The weather is too bad in January and February to do anything but sit inside and watch the tube. Do you have any idea how many college basketball games are televised during January and February? Eating just goes with watching college basketball on television.

Carrot and celery sticks don't exactly do justice to the game, either. We're talking chips and dip. Lots of chips and dip.

Start my diet in March? Forget it. The Road to the Final Four is paved with chicken wings and salsa.

Easter comes in April. No use starting a diet and having to break it on Easter Sunday. Might as well wait until after Spring Break. Isn't that when the Girl Scout cookies are delivered?

Now every May, I do make progress. I'm thinking about going to the beach and putting on a bathing suit, so I eat pretzels and watch the Braves. I even start walking a mile or two every day.

But May is followed by June and July and summer is such a great time for cookouts. Hard to lose weight on a diet of t-bone steak and ribs, not to mention hamburgers and barbecued chicken. We certainly travel during those months, and nobody diets on vacation. August is Camp Meeting month, which means hearty meals and homemade ice cream every night. It's a wonder I don't weigh more than I do.

But this time I'm serious. I've carried this weight around for 14 years, and when I sit down to my Thanksgiving dinner, I intend to be thankful that there is at least thirty pounds less of me to feed. Starting today, September 1, I am on a strict diet. I'll keep you posted concerning my progress.

Of course, Saturday is Georgia's home opener and there are several tail gate parties I'm expected to attend. Monday is Labor Day. No school. We will probably have a fish fry in the noon hour and a barbecue Monday evening.

Well, next Tuesday, I'm going on a diet. And this time I really mean it!

Is There a Lawyer in the House?

After this article appeared, the paper got a letter from an irate reader who insisted that Ben Matlock wore seersucker suits. After weeks of investigation I finally drove to the Andy Griffith museum in Mt. Airy, NC where they have one of the Matlock suits on display. I must admit, it may not be linen, but that sucker definitely ain't seersucker,

I've been wondering lately why lawyers get such a bad rap. People snicker when you mention the word attorney. The internet has entire web sites devoted to lawyer jokes. Oglethorpe wrote in the original Georgia charter that they should be permanently banned from the colony. If you believe everything you read, lawyers are the personification of evil.

They couldn't be all that bad, could they? Luckily, I've not been involved in many legal entanglements but I do know several members of the bar and they seem like regular folks. The ones I know have wives and go to baseball and soccer games on Saturday, just like the rest of us.

I'm sure some of them even go to church on Sunday. In fact, two members of my Sunday School class are lawyers. I've never seen them steal from the offering plate and when fellow class members ask for prayers because they've been in a car wreck or something, I've never seen either of them hand out a business card, at least not inside the church.

My first cousin is an attorney in Covington and he's not so bad. In fact, I was called to sit on a jury for one of his cases and he told the judge right away that we were kin. Of course, he was under oath.

My wife's cousin married a lady lawyer and she asked me to photograph the wedding. She bought lots of pictures and never once mentioned suing me because one of her bridesmaid was overexposed in a few shots.

So where do all the complaints about lawyers come from?

Can't blame it on a right wing conspiracy. Someone else already has that excuse.

Maybe it's because attorneys, by the very nature of their business, spend a lot of time with criminals. What's that old saying about guilt by association? " If you lie down with dogs, you get up with fleas?"

It couldn't be John Grisham novels. Lawyers already had a bad reputation before *The Firm* became popular.

I guess that leaves television to blame. Maybe people have a negative image of lawyers because so many are portrayed as unscrupulous and a bit greedy on television shows. I don't know a habeus from a corpus but I have to admit that there are a few shows about the law profession that I enjoy watching on TV.

One of my favorite shows, in fact, is Ally McBeal. She is a skinny little thing who wears real short skirts and works in a Boston law firm, along with several very weird characters, including her ex-lover and his current wife. Her roommate works for the DA's office and usually winds up facing her in court. Her firm's office is right over a nightclub, which is convenient, because everyone winds up there drinking and dancing after every case.

The most unusual feature of the office is the unisex bathroom where all sorts of drama takes place, but not before everyone gets down on the floor to check under the stalls for eavesdroppers. The show is a bit off the wall and I'm not sure why I like it so much. My wife insists it's because the star's skirts are so short, but there must be a deeper meaning. If the practice of law was as much fun as Ally McBeal makes it seem, I'd sue somebody every week.

I know one thing. Ally McBeal could never work for Perry Mason. Remember him? He defended a murder case every week. It's a wonder there was anyone left in Los Angeles to kill by the time O.J. came along. Perry had a loyal secretary named Della Street, but they were never, to my knowledge, alone in the same bathroom. Paul Drake was Mason's private detective and always got sent away to places like Las Vegas to track down the real killer while Perry Mason stayed around to argue with Lt. Tragg of homicide.

Not only did Perry Mason always get his client off the hook, he always shamed or tricked the real murderer into admitting his or her guilt by blurting a confession with five minutes left in the show, which gave Perry, Paul, and Della, just enough time to go back to his office for a cigarette. Guess he never thought of renting space over a nightclub.

My favorite television attorney of all time, though, would have to be Ben Matlock. For those of you who may not know it, after Opie was grown, his daddy moved from Mayberry to Atlanta, changed his name to Matlock and hung out his shingle. He was like a down-home Perry Mason. He had a closet full of identical white linen suits and celebrated all his victories by eating two hotdogs with everything. That's healthier than smoking, but not as much fun as dancing.

So what's the truth about lawyers and the practice of law? Are most lawyers as upright and boring as the ones I know, or as glamorous and daring as the ones on television? My guess is that, like everyone else, they're somewhere in between. And if I've slandered or libeled anyone with this column—I plead the Fifth.

Of Blind Dates and Other Matters of the Heart

This piece is dedicated to James T. Milligan, one of the funniest human beings I know, and the one person in the world who told more people about my date with "Aunt Bea" than I did.

I was standing around in a parking lot the other night. When you have three kids with half a dozen activities each, you spend a lot of time standing around in parking lots. This happened to be the church parking lot on a Sunday night.

Several of us parent/chauffeur types were waiting on MYF to be over and the conversation turned to points of origin. (We got to talking about where we were raised.) Naturally a chorus of "Did you know so and so?" began. One person in the crowd happened to mention having had a blind date with a girl someone else knew. We were off, full throttle, down memory lane. Each person had a better blind date story than the last.

I said nothing. Most of my blind date experiences were too painful to recount, even in the church parking lot.

Upon returning home, however, I started thinking about some of them. Honesty compels me to admit that there were many, as I was almost thirty before I met my wife, Lisa. Our meeting, courtship, and subsequent marriage, of course, put an end to all of my dating, blind or otherwise.

I don't think I ever had a blind date in high school, but I did get "fixed up" a few times in college. On a couple of those occasions I wound up wishing that I were blind. Ever the gentleman, I never let on that I was disappointed. Besides, I was smart enough to know that my companion of the evening never opened her door and felt like she had won the lottery, either.

I don't mean to sound insensitive here. I know that beauty is only skin deep, but as any college aged male will tell you, ugly goes all the way to the bone. One date in particular stands out in my mind. She was the only true two-bagger I've ever met. You've heard, I'm sure, the old colloquialism about a date being so homely you'd need to put a bag over her head to take her out in public. With a two bagger, you put a bag over your head, too, just in case hers falls off. This was that girl. It was the only time in my life that I just bolted and ran.

Now I know what some of you are thinking, and no, I don't judge books by their covers. I know that looks aren't what is important. I also know that while a car runs on gas, it takes a spark to get it started.

Some of the blind dates I had in college turned out to be very pretty, but dumb as a box of rocks. I took a history major from a large Southern university to Stone Mountain and she wanted to know who those guys on horses were, carved into the side of the rock. Another sweet young thing, from deep south Georgia, was confused when we went to see a movie starring Robert Redford because she was certain she had seen him killed in Butch Cassidy and the Sundance Kid, back at the drive-in in Cuthbert.

Once I graduated from college, blind dates became even more frequent. People just seemed to worry about a guy in his twenties who was not married. I went out with cousins, sisters, aunts, school teachers—all of whom were billed as sweet, fun to be with, and having great personalities. The results were never good, but for some reason, I kept getting fixed up. Until I met Aunt Bea.

I was living in a trailer in a pecan grove in Meigs, Georgia. It's 7 miles north of Ochlocknee and 12 miles southwest of Cotton. A friend from Covington was also serving time in South Georgia and living in Albany. His wife, knowing I was a stranger in a strange land, called one evening. She had the perfect person for me to meet. I should have known better, but being alone in Meigs, Georgia does strange things to a young man's mind.

I called this perfect person on the phone. She sounded nice enough and we made a date for dinner and a movie. I drove the thirty miles to her apartment, found her unit, and knocked on the door.

The person who answered my knock was the spitting image of Aunt Bea, from the Andy Griffith Show. She had the same face, the same frumpy house dress, and the same hairdo. I was in a state of shock, but running was not an option.

We drove around Albany until I found a restaurant that looked deserted. She ordered liver and onions. We then went to the worst movie house in the city to see the worst movie. She grabbed my hand as soon as the house lights went down and refused to let go. The feature lasted three hours. It seemed like twelve. As we finally left the show my worst fears were realized. Two teachers from my school were in the lobby. I had to acknowledge them. To their credit, they smiled and said nothing more than hello.

That is, until the next day. When I arrived at school the next morning they were both in my room to greet me. "We have only one question," they said. "Who baby-sat Opie last night?"

I was cured. I never went on another blind date. In fact, I met Lisa shortly after that. She looks nothing like Aunt Bea, so when she asked me out I quickly said, "yes." We've been together ever since.

But if you're ever in Albany and see a nice lady with a beehive hairdo, eating liver and onions in a nice restaurant—tell her Gomer says "Hey!"

Is Walt's Wonderful World About to Be Gone With the Ratings Wind?

For a while after this book went to press, Tinkerbell still still lit up Cinderella's castle every Sunday night. But, alas, no more.

You can't believe everything you read in the newspapers. This may come as a shock to some of you, but just because it's in the newspapers doesn't mean that it's the gospel truth. I'm not talking about this newspaper, of course. I'm referring to all those other newspapers out there.

We all remember seeing the picture of Harry Truman holding up the front page of the Chicago Daily Tribune with big headlines saying, "Dewey Wins." Problem was, all the votes hadn't been counted. Dewey didn't win.

Last week I read in the AJC that Georgia was going to upset Tennessee. Believe me. Dewey did much better against Truman than Georgia did against Tennessee.

Newspapers are full of stories that might or might not be

true. I hope the story I read last week is not. According to the headline, ABC is contemplating taking the *Wonderful World of Disney* off the air after the current season. Say it ain't so!

Those Sunday night shows are one of the last remaining ties to my childhood. Everything else seems to have gone the way of the hula hoop and Coca Cola in little green bottles. Sears-Roebuck doesn't even have a Christmas Wish Book anymore. And now we may lose Walt Disney on Sunday nights.

My whole family used to gather in front of the television on Sunday nights, anxious to discover what wonders Mr. Disney had in store for us. He would always appear, you remember, at the beginning of the program to introduce the show. He would be in a room full of books in front of a giant world globe. When I was a child I remember thinking it would be like dying and going to heaven to have a room like that.

Walt Disney would chat for a while and then walk over and take a book off the shelf. He would open it up and a story would magically come to life. Sometimes Jiminy Crickett, with a top hat and umbrella, would pop out of the book. Sometimes it would be cartoon features with Mickey Mouse, Donald, Pluto, Goofy, and the gang. Disney presented nature studies long before Marlin Perkins. Sometimes he would choose a history book from the shelf. Those were my favorite shows. I believe that my love for history is due, at least in part, to the shows Walt Disney presented on Sunday night.

The stories might not have been historically accurate, but they aroused my interest, and made me want to learn more. Johnny Tremain taught me how the American Revolution began. The Swamp Fox showed me how the war was fought in our part of the world.

I didn't like watching the Civil War shows, *The Great Locomotive Chase* and the *Drummer Boy of Shiloh*. The wrong side always won. Without a doubt, my favorite Sunday night Disney Serial was *Davy Crockett, King of the Wild Frontier.* Week after week I followed Davy and Georgie Russell from the hills of Tennessee all the way to the Alamo. I still can't walk into one of those gift shops in the mountains without trying on one of the fake coonskin caps and begging my wife to take my picture.

Of course, the same actors played all the characters. Fess Parker was the Swamp Fox and Davy Crockett. He even played the Yankee spy in the Great Locomotive Chase. Took me years to forgive him for that. Tim Consodine was a regular and so was Kevin Cochran, who played a little boy named Moochie. Don't even start me thinking about Annette.

Some weeks the show would feature Disneyland, in California. Central Florida was still swamp land and orange groves at this time. I remember staring in amazement at all the rides and attractions. I never in a million years dreamed that I would be able to actually see such a place.

At some point the show changed its name to *Walt Disney's Wonderful World of Color*. Tinkerbell, Peter Pan's fairy friend, would fly over Cinderella's castle and wave her magic wand. At that point the screen would, supposedly, turn into a world of color. It stayed the same on our set. By the time we had a color television I had found other things to do on Sunday night and left Walt Disney to others. I rediscovered the show when I had kids of my own.

We're not as faithful to the current show as my family was. Let's face it. We have a hundred channels now instead of three and Michael Eisenwhoever is no Walt Disney. The bill of fare is wholesome family movies these days, and who wants to watch wholesome family movies when there's so much trash available? I think Whoopie Goldberg has taken Annette's job.

Although the Walt Disney Corporation is a giant conglomerate with making money it's prime objective, it still creates magnificent family entertainment and gives my kids a chance to laugh at the same things I did. If it disappears from television another part of what was good about my generation's childhood will go with it.

I hope ABC changes it's mind. I like watching the show, especially the beginning. Tinkerbell still waves her wand over the castle and now I have a color television.

"Pork Skin Diet"
Ends on Thanksgiving Day

The Atkins Diet worked wonders. I lost 35 pounds eating bacon, eggs, steak--and pork skins. I went off the diet on Thanksgiving. By Ground Hogs Day I had gained 40 pounds back.

A couple of months ago I boldly announced that I was going on a strict diet. I had good intentions of doing just that, too. Of course we all know that good intentions pave the path to you know where.

I tried. I really did. But there was just too much good stuff out there to eat. I live in a house with three kids who are junk food addicts and a wife who could eat Hosea William's entire "Feed the Hungry" larder and not gain an ounce. By the time September turned to October I had gained three more pounds and David Hays, cotton farmer turned land developer, was openly making fun of my protruding belly.

On October 16, fate intervened in the ongoing battle of the Huckaby bulge. Lisa and I hosted a Sunday school party at our house. The entertainment for the evening was provided by the football teams from the state universities of Georgia and Tennessee. For the hundredth straight year the orange team volunteered to kick my team all the way back to Athens. It was a great night if "Rocky Top" is your favorite song.

However, the night was not a total loss. While I was stuffing my face with chicken wings, salsa, potato chips and onion dip, several rather svelte members of my class were telling me about an amazing new diet they had discovered. It was actually an old diet that had been reintroduced by a doctor somewhere named Atkins. My friends explained to me that the diet was an all protein, no carbohydrate thing in which you can eat all the bacon, cheese, and t-bone steaks you can force down your gullet, but no ice cream, pasta, or refined sugar.

It sounded too good to be true. I filled a tortilla chip with bean dip and asked about snacks. "Cheese," was the first response from my new found weight loss gurus. Not too appetizing for me.

Then someone said that I could eat all the peanuts I wanted. Someone else added, "and pork rinds." I think they meant the last remark as a joke. It was actually the selling point. My wife hasn't let me have a pork skin in the 17 years we've been married.

"It's a done deal!" I promised, "as soon as I finish that coconut pie I have out in the refrigerator."

The next day we began. I say we because my lovely wife Lisa, who has to run around in the shower to get wet, was as enthusiastic about the possibilities of my losing weight as David Hays and my Sunday school class. She went out and bought me the "Dr. Atkins Diet Revolution" book, three dozen eggs, ten pounds of bacon, a dozen ribeye steaks, and 32 cans of dry roasted peanuts. I was ready to go.

The first three days on my pork rind diet went well. I ate huge amounts of bacon, eggs, cheese, and hamburger steak, without the slightest twinge of guilt. Amazingly enough, I actually lost two pounds. After four days my body began to tremble a little bit, so Lisa brought home a car load of vitamins to replace the nutrients I wasn't getting. The trembling stopped.

For a week or so, the diet was fun. What a novelty! I could turn the prescribed food pyramid upside down and eat like a pig, as long as I stayed away from anything healthy. After the first week, although the pounds were falling off, I started having nearly uncontrollable cravings for mashed potatoes and rice. It was of little consolation that I could eat all the butter and mayonnaise I wanted, because there was absolutely nothing to put them on. I did discover, however, that French onion dip goes real well with pork skins. At night I began to dream about white bread and sweet iced tea.

When my friends were singing the praises of all the wonderful things I could have, they never mentioned all the things I wouldn't be able to eat. Some things you don't appreciate until you can't have them.

Like orange juice. Who would ever think orange juice would be banned from a diet, along with toast, grapefruit, apples, oranges, and bananas? Forget about a bowl of cereal in the morning. Milk either, for that matter. Pretend grits do not exist.

Lunch is a salad. That's it. But with all the Italian dressing you can pour on that sucker.

Dinner is any type of meat and some cabbage. No corn bread, black eyed peas, potatoes, rice, pasta, rolls, sweet tea, or anything else that wasn't available to cave men. I wonder why Fred Flintstone wasn't as skinny as a rail.

I vowed to stay on the diet until Thanksgiving. So far I have. At the five week mark I have lost 25 pounds, from 215 to 190, and taken my belt up two notches. I've even gotten compliments on how much better I look. The jury is still out as to whether it has been worth it. I do feel better and haven't dreamed about white bread in a couple of weeks.

But let me tell you this. I'm going back to the real world of sugars and starches on Thanksgiving Day. When they put my mama's dressing and sweet potato pie on the table, everybody had better stand back. What's left of me could hurt somebody!

E-Mail Address Opens New Can of Worms

After this column appeared I was besieged by even more e-mail. I'd like to hear from you, too, but don't send anything after 9:30 at night. I go to bed early.

My column has appeared in this space for over a year now. During that time I have developed a very good working relation with the paper's editor, Alice Queen. The relationship works like this: She tells me what to do and I do it. It was easy for me to get in the swing of things here at the newspaper. That's the exact same arrangement I have with my wife, Lisa.

A few weeks ago, Alice and I had a discussion about whether I should add an e-mail address to the bottom of my column. I discovered the internet, quite by accident, two summers ago and found out that while it may be as addictive as heroin it is cheap and nonfattening, so it's one of the few vices Lisa allows me to enjoy.

My discussion with Alice over adding my address to my column went something like this:

Alice: "I want you to start putting your e-mail address at the end of your column so we don't have to keep spending money forwarding all your mail to your house. It cost the paper 33 cents last month!

Me: "Yes ma'am."

So now I have an e-mail address at the end of my column and all the people who are too lazy or too cheap or too illiterate to send me a real letter can just log on to the old internet and fire away. Boy, they have, too. I thought it might be fun to share some of the more interesting comments.

One thing I have noticed is that people have some really strange screen names. I state my opinions week after week in this forum. Not only my name but also my picture accompanies my opinion. I'm not afraid to take a stand on such controversial issues as barbecue and catfish and the Confederate flag. I state my case and let the chips fall where they may. These people who e-mail me use names like Bubbasbuddy006 and Bigmamagal807. It's easy to be brave under a pseudonym like IAMClassless417.

Many of my critics have rather long memories, too, because I have gotten response this week concerning columns that ran months ago. Talk about carrying a grudge. I haven't had a chance to respond personally to my e-mails so, if you will indulge me, I'll just answer in this space.

From JoiseyGal911: Dear Mr. Huckaby. I resemble your

remarks about Yankees moving to the South. If you had to listen to New Jersey accents twelve months a year, you'd come south, too.

Dear JoiseyGal. I don't mind your coming here. It's the staying that bothers me.

From ImaHogg: Dear Dummy. How can you say that Sprayberry's has the best barbecue. I'm an expert on pork and I can tell you about a dozen places better than Sprayberry's.

Dear Ima. I'll tell you the same thing I told the woman who said she knew of better catfish than Henderson's. Don't tell me—take me. I'm like Delta. I'm ready when you are.

From RollTide006. Huckaby. iffen you thinks all the teachers in ga is so great, how come is it that my boy Cecil done had to spend three years in the same grade when we get him to school at least twict a week.

Dear Roll: I can't understand it either. That's a real mystery to me.

From JohnnyReb1861: Dear Mr. Huckaby. How can you write that the Confederate battle flag should be taken off our state banner. You are just an ignorant, liberal, Yankee-loving traitor to the South. How can you live with yourself after writing rubbish like that?

Dear Johnny. Sometimes I do get really sad. When I do, I either go outside and kick our cat, Sherman-Grant, or I sit by the fire and read the obituaries from the New York Times.

From JRocker 49. Dear Mr. Huckaby. I read your very patriotic Veteran's Day column about all the men who died protecting our Constitution and Bill of Rights. Could you go over that part about Free Speech and Freedom of Expression one more time?

Dear John. Certainly. As soon as I get through explaining to PRose14 why doing drugs a gazillion times is not as bad as gambling.

From PattyPrude111. Dear Mr. Huckaby. I was appalled that you would tell someone to "kiss your rebel rump." You should be ashamed of yourself. How could you use a word like rump in this newspaper?

Dear Patty. Actually I didn't use the word rump. The editor did. I used a much more descriptive word, which reminds me of a story I once heard about President Harry Truman. His press secretary approached his wife one day and implored, "Mrs. Truman, can't you please get the president to stop using the word manure in his speeches?"

The First Lady replied, "Sir, you don't understand. It's taken me fifteen years to get the President *to* use the word manure."

From Blindandcrookedref666. I told you Georgia was gonna lose to Tech.

Dear Blind and crooked. I don't want to talk about it. (But he didn't fumble.)

From Flirtyone: I really like the picture of you on the front of the paper, but doesn't your wife complain about your beard tickling her face when you kiss.

Dear Flirty. It's really never come up. I've only had my beard six years.

I think that just about catches me up on this week's correspondence. Y'all keep those e-mails coming.

Darrell Huckaby
DHuck08@bellsouth.net
www.darrellhuckaby.net

Other Great Books by
Darrell Huckaby

Need Two

Dinner on the Grounds

Southern Is as Southern Does

Hard Rock to Solid Rock

Need Four

What the Huck!

For info on all these titles--or to order--visit
Huck's general store at:

www.darrellhuckaby.net

Printed in the United States
97557LV00004B/214-261/A